Christianity versus Fatalistic Religions in the War Against Poverty

Christianity versus Fatalistic Religions in the War Against Poverty

UDO MIDDELMANN

Paternoster:
thinking faith

COLORADO SPRINGS · MILTON KEYNES · HYDERABAD

Paternoster Publishing
We welcome your questions and comments.

USA	1820 Jet Stream Drive, Colorado Springs, CO 80921
	www.authenticbooks.com
UK	9 Holdom Avenue, Bletchley, Milton Keynes, Bucks, MK1 1QR
	www.authenticmedia.co.uk
India	Logos Bhavan, Medchal Road, Jeedimetla Village, Secunderabad 500 055, A.P.

Christianity versus Fatalistic Religions in the War against Poverty
ISBN-13: 978-1-934068-28-1
ISBN-10: 1-934068-28-4

Copyright © 2007 by Udo Middelmann

10 09 08 / 6 5 4 3 2 1

Published in 2008 by Paternoster, a division of Authentic
All rights reserved. No part of this book may be reproduced in any form without permission in writing from the publisher, except in the case of brief quotations embodied in critical articles or reviews.

All Scripture quotations, unless otherwise indicated, are taken from the *Holy Bible, New International Version*®. *NIV*®. Copyright © 1973, 1978, 1984 by International Bible Society. Used by permission of Zondervan. All rights reserved.

A catalog record for this book is available from the Library of Congress.

Cover and interior design: projectluz.com
Editorial team: Bette Smyth, Dan Johnson, Dana Bromley

Printed in the United States of America

Contents

Introduction ... 1

Chapter 1
Water and Worldviews ... 17

Chapter 2
Bread, Fish, and a Better Focus ... 41

Chapter 3
A Community of Character ... 69

Chapter 4
Servants' Hearts and Skills ... 95

Chapter 5
Worldviews in Collision ... 123

Chapter 6
Ethics in the Circle of Life ... 147

Chapter 7
Gutsy Christians ... 171

Chapter 8
The Samaritan Appeal ... 191

Postscript ... 209

Introduction

The whole encounter was initially quite amusing to us. He, however, lost his job over a failed attempt to send us away.

We had just landed in the small capital of one of the northern regions, or *oblasts*, of the former Soviet Union in the dead of winter. Before a second plane even arrived with the rest of our team and materials, the lone man in coat and hat at the foot of the steps of our plane had started to plead with us to return immediately to Moscow.

We were no longer welcome in this forested region. The governor had changed his mind and now wanted us to leave at once. The invitation to hold a conference was rescinded.

This was the early nineties, and the tension in town between politicians and educators, between local authorities and foreign guests, between Orthodox churchmen and possible heretics from the West had scared him. The best solution would be for us to just disappear. The exposure of local habits to outside observation and possible scrutiny was too much to risk. At best, it would be a novel experiment with an uncertain outcome.

Besides that, had not Moscow previously imposed on this region a seminar for teachers? And now with local autonomy awakened, suspicion about Moscow's central planning added salt to the painful realization that we had actually arrived at the airport.

And then the second plane landed. We negotiated briefly, informing the man with the hat that we had firm reservations in a local hotel, that the planes had other scheduled obligations, and that we would stay at least one night and try to understand the reasons for the sudden change of plans.

I traveled all over the former Soviet Union in the early nineties, speaking at teacher-training seminars on subjects as diverse as "Universal Human Rights" and "Christianity as a Foundation for a Moral Society." Large groups of teachers, administrators, and education officials gathered for four or five days at a time in the capitals of almost every one of the eighty-four provinces, oblasts, and semi-independent republics over the span of years from 1991 to 1997.

Introduction

The seminars were organized by the Ministry of Education in Moscow in the hope of encouraging teachers to add classes and subjects to their education program. Besides the already rich offerings in sports, arts, ballet, orchestra, and crafts, our materials offered access to studies in philosophy, Christianity, and literature.

After the demise of Marxism as a controlling philosophy of life and in the face of a cultural, moral, and economic vacuum, our seminars aimed at opening the discussion on alternative worldviews. These seminars challenged the previous monopoly of views and brought forth questions that had been suppressed for years. Neither the state party nor the belief in the answers limited to scientific materialism had allowed any space for inquiry. Following the inhumanities committed in the name of an "inevitable scientific" progress, a concern for human life, thought, and creativity would now be stressed. Personal responsibility would replace collective guilt or innocence, depending on your point of view.

In my lectures I would point out that a truly educated person knows the basics of biblical teaching and its intellectual, moral, and social importance to society, even if for no other reason than to understand Western thought and culture. Its museums, systems of law, the balance of power in government, the priority of human life, entrepreneurship, the concept of personal responsibility, and social services—even the very idea of humanism itself—all result from the teachings of the Bible. These ideas had over many centuries and during many generations gradually transformed a pagan, fatalistic, and backward continent into what it is today. Emigrants of all professions took these ideas as seeds with them and planted them around the world.

Our lectures, seminars, small-group sessions, and study materials revealed how different these teachings are from the influence of religion. Christianity relates to the real world, not to a world of false faith and make-believe. Of course, the Bible starts with the Creator, but then it describes the wonder and tragedy of human history and its resolution through the continuing investment of God in human beings.

We knew that every educated Russian had gone through the compulsory class on scientific atheism. Religion had been presented as an opiate that keeps people tied to patterns without much change and discourages any effort to deal with the real problems in people's lives. It was easy for us to agree with that low view of religion. But we also pointed to parallels in the Russian world of faith with its emphasis on denial: denial of the body, denial of real suffering, and denial of the mind. This type of faith pursues a spiritual existence that makes the believer "float" above the daily problems of hunger, pain, and the need to understand things and people.

The Bible deals instead with questions about reality that have arisen for most people in any cultural or religious setting from their childhood on, throughout human history. These questions concern life and death, good and evil, and right and wrong. They deal with authority and doubt and with the individual and relationships to the group. They question history as being either cyclical or linear. And they wonder about where it all started: Is there one God, are there many gods, or is everything a mere flow of energy in some form or another? Finally, all people question whether everything is normal or abnormal and, therefore, whether our response should be repetition or change.

Against the protest of the little welcoming committee of one, we settled in and then went to meet with the governor. We heard his objections and promised not to talk about religion or to be "missionaries." We were told that all our sessions would have "observers" to check on our compliance. We would be asked to leave if we failed to keep our side of the agreement.

As the conference started, it soon became obvious who the observers were: women with more makeup than was appropriate showed up in sessions led by male leaders, and men in standard gray suits were in all other groups. As long as observers were present, participants in the groups would barely speak. We kept to our bargain and presented ideas and materials in an altered form and vocabulary. We also took turns, however, inviting the observers out for tea, personal conversation, and other genuine distractions away from the group to give greater freedom of expression to the interested teachers.

After the first plenary session in the morning, I went to lunch in one of the assigned schools in town. A man in recognizable government-issue gray sat alone at a table, and I joined him there. When a translator arrived, I asked the official which school he came from and what subject he taught. He responded that he was not a teacher, and I warmly said, "You must be one of the observers then." He did not seem very pleased by this quick discovery of his assigned role.

I asked whether he liked what he had heard. "Yes, but I don't like religion," he said. I took his hand to shake it and said, with genuine enthusiasm, that I could not agree with him more. "I also think that religion is a damaging thing. Just look at India under the influence of Hinduism or Africa under the weight of tribal religions. Religions keep people in bondage, backward in development, and irresponsible."

He was very surprised at my statement. I continued to explain that what people need is an explanation of the real world and an affirmation of their own value, which are the concepts that gave rise to the more human and better cultural and economic conditions in what people call the Western world. That is the result of a biblical view of life, not of religion. I continued with something like this: "When you read the Bible and use it as a pair of glasses, you will see reality, including human beings, life and death, and work and culture in a way that corresponds to the way people already experience these things. In addition, the Bible places the human being in the center of its attention, though not in the center of the universe. God is the eternal person; he is not just some form of energy. Certainly, people are not eternal, because they have not always existed. But they are unique, and since they will exist forever, their lives, choices, and personalities really matter. The Bible addresses human beings, not animals or angels. Human beings are central there, and their lives, their choices, their woes and pains really matter for two reasons. First, human beings are made in the image of God and are not accidents of nature or mere bundles of energy forces. Second, humans have a serious problem that does not originate in their personalities, their minds, or their bodies. The reason things don't work right lies in Adam's rejection of God's authority and our continuing down the same path. Now we humans pretend to be God and fail at it, and the universe falls on top of us."

By the end of our seminar we had collected from among us a year's salary to give to the official whose failure to send us packing resulted in the loss of his job. On an open microphone many teachers spoke of their joy in rediscovering in Christianity the human face, soul, and life—ideas that were once known in Russian intellectual and cultural circles and that Marxism had repressed for seventy years.

Different worldviews work like different sets of glasses. Some paint everything brown or pink. Most worldview glasses let us see reality only as a big blur, which makes it virtually impossible to recognize the dangers in it. Other glasses let us look only through a thin slit, which keeps us from seeing what hazards lurk around the side. None of these allows us to walk without stumbling as we try to find our way around the world.

What we need is not a set of glasses that paints a pretty picture or one that everyone agrees with. We need glasses that put reality into focus. We need to see more clearly and recognize the sharp edges of reality.

The world is a dangerous place. Nature is indifferent to our needs, and not all neighbors are kind and supportive. We cannot fail to carefully observe whether our glasses reveal or distort. We need to compare what we notice through them with the sights and experiences of others. Some people may have to change glasses to stop stumbling over curbs and into holes. Some may have to remove their shades to observe true colors, real people, and dangers around the corner.

When we wear the glasses of false religions, we tend to become tied to impersonal nature (everything is matter, energy, and forces) or to powerful personal gods (everything is spiritual, faith, and submission). Both of these views tie people into a bundle with death, not life. Repetitive formulas and practices will explain away all the ups and downs of life by advocating some kind of master plan to be followed, a plan in which all events have their assigned place and purpose.

Introduction

It is hard to wear these glasses consistently, for human beings seek to create alternative explanations. We question and complain, we doubt, and we want to improve by trying something new. We want to burst our limitations of space and time. While this is mainly a good habit, it also contains the seeds for two problems. First, it may elevate the pursuit of an idea to the level of assumed truth. Such ideologies bring great harm, for they are not linked to possibilities in the real world. Second, it will bring us into conflict with most religions, which tell us to lie low and accept the inevitable on our path to an inevitable death.

Religion says that it is a mistake to see ourselves as human beings, as individuals with moral judgments and distinct values. Religion does not encourage human aspirations along proper channels. Instead it seeks to make us drowsy, like a drug. It seeks to kill the sensation of pain rather than to deal with it objectively. For example, after a lecture a number of years ago in New Delhi, a teacher in the audience told me, "With our religion we each try to find a way to resolve life's frequent tensions and to reduce pain. All religions seek a way to make sense of life and to find peace in order to face death."

I believe that he was correct and that he spoke for most people in their various cultural, historical, and geographical settings. For generations, people living in the Swiss valleys revere the mountains that threaten them as well as shelter them from outsiders. Mountains protect their fields from cold northern winds, while creating harsh conditions and frequent avalanches. In order to accept this cycle as unalterable, death is seen as part of everyone's climb toward the light, the sun, and the universal "everything." The loss of individuality and distinction is the core belief, and death is the release and resting place, the end of the life experienced now.

African villagers reconstruct their round houses with leaves and straw each time tropical weather or termites weaken the structures enough for them to collapse. Nomadic herdsmen in Mongolia watch their flocks day and night throughout the year, experiencing life's cycles—the annual seasons and the birth and death of all things. South American peasants live in fear of the spirits they worship. Marxists in Russia see a redemptive role in bowing to an inevitable progress that advances through struggle and conflict: the formidable scientific interaction of energy among the vastness of the stars in space, among particles in tiny atoms, and among classes of human beings struggling against each other.

Beautiful photographs bring people with these beliefs and various practices into our living rooms. The rhythm of the year here, the rites of passage there, the struggle for greater feelings of peace within fixed communal behavior patterns, and the conquest of power through physics—such human interactions with the world around us seek harmony, belonging, purpose, and the rhyme and reason for life. But

Introduction

these pictures do not usually reveal the dark side of reality: its painful contradictions, class struggles, cultural revolutions, extermination camps, and genocide—the whole reality of hard punches and large bruises that are part of human history and an untidy nature.

Most cultures—and behind them, most religions—whether spiritual and mystical or secular and materialist, offer a measure of security in patterns, repetitions, and submission. Pain, injustice, and death itself are diminished by either normalizing or denying their realities through disciplined attitudes and group behavior.

Religion expresses how people relate to the bigger world, the universe, and the powers that control the unrolling of history. Religion describes ways to fit in, to submit, to explain away, to live in community, and to share in a social collective both joy and sorrow, both help and horror.

Religion's main effort seems to be to rid the person of individual freedom and derived sovereignty. Religion is an invitation and a path to denial. Individuals can either deny that there are real problems or deny that personal perceptions are important. Religion maintains that whatever happens is normal and unavoidable, ubiquitous and repetitive, and part of the plan of nature or god.

Religion answers Goethe's question about the contrast between the atrocities of the French Revolution in 1789 and the quality of the Sicilian wine in the same year by insisting that Goethe should just accept the facts. He should stop being curious or even troubled. Asking such questions leads to no answers. Buddha's search for detachment from the contrasting experiences of joy and sorrow, youth and age, birth and death is his answer to the tension we all feel. Religion demands blind faith and conformity.

There is little difference in the basic approach to life between the mystical religion of Islam and the materialist religion of the naturalist or Marxist. Both understand that life in all its parts is inevitable, necessary, and part of the program, whether that is rooted in Islam's God or nature's energy, in fate, or in the flow of history. Yet all human beings raise questions and attempt to resist this loss of the human spirit. Religions dunk us under water while our human spirits seek to breathe and try to keep our heads above it.

Into this bleak situation thunders the provocative proposition of the Bible: "In the beginning God. . . . In the beginning was the Word" (Genesis 1:1; John 1:1). God—a thinking, feeling, creating personality—engages himself with the human being whom he made in his image and who is unlike all the rest of what he created. The human mind is addressed in language; creativity is mandated and demanded in an unfinished and open world; understanding is essential to examine the content of the text for its truthful correspondence to reality at any moment of history and to distinguish it from lies, propaganda, and deception.

Introduction

The collapse of the former Soviet Union was the result of various internal factors contributing to the breakdown of the wall in Berlin. What power could dismantle weapons of furious destructive potential and bring to life again sensitivity, emotions, and the arts? The focus on heavy industry, material power, and the military had blinded many in Russia to the power of words and ideas, except as state propaganda. The Helsinki agreement in 1977 on finalizing European borders after World War II gave Moscow the material security it craved for Russia. The price it paid was the free flow of ideas through cultural and scientific exchanges, investigative journalism, jazz music, and foreign radio broadcasts. Material security was gained at the expense of information and ideas. Moscow believed in the power of propaganda but not in the power of more accurate information from and about the outside world.

Subsequently, a multitude of other ideas and accessible information reached a wider population. These were ideas about life, human beings, individuals, creativity, scientific research, social responsibilities, and about resisting fate, nature, bad government, and death itself. The picture of an inevitable march of history through class struggle was replaced by personal possibilities. Propaganda about the world outside was dismantled through pictures, travel, and experiences from the outside world.

When biblical Christianity took a stand against the cacophony of other religions, it drove the accused imperialists to greater humanity. Whereas religions drug people into submission and, at times, stupidity, Christianity energizes mind and body to creative action. Religions still serve as the opiate of the people and contribute to human, intellectual, and economic poverty in many parts of the world. But the teachings of the Bible have contributed massively to positive cultural consequences, in a broad sense, in all Western countries and where they were carried abroad. Belief in the God of the Bible has led to significant—though never perfect—practices of biblical ethics, human rights, intellectual development, and individual and social responsibilities that have had visible consequences in the material realm.

Every worldview directs people and their lives, but only the biblical perspective provides an accurate view of reality that also satisfies the inquisitive mind.

Compared with other cultures, wherever Jewish and Christian thought has been checked against reality and been found true, people have made greater strides in mastering a hostile world and controlling abusive power through democratic procedures, self-discipline, and education. The spiritual and intellectual climate that the Bible introduces results in a highly functional view of God and humans, of work and life, and of individuals and society. More than just a view or perspective, the Bible has influenced the way people have lived, loved, and labored. Biblically influenced societies, in general, have been able to more effectively fight disease, reduce hunger, and restrain human and natural evil.

The Bible's statement that "man does not live on bread alone but on every word that comes from the mouth of the Lord" (Deuteronomy 8:3) is both an admonition and an encouragement. It states an obligation of the creature to the Creator. At the same time, it is an invitation to listen to him who knows creation best, for he made it in a certain way. The Creator defines the shape of things he made, demands a humane ethic of love and respect, and calls for moral action and substantial healing that exposes sin, evil, and destruction in the reality of a fallen world.

The clues for life are not found in *what is* but in what *ought to be*, as it is set out in words and images. Nature is not our mother; instead, we trust a Father in heaven. Death is not merely a statistic or a natural event, but an obscene enemy.

Above all physical power and human politics are the concerns of right and wrong, of morality. Abolition of slavery, defining women's rights, making time for a real childhood, safer work conditions and precise norms, definitions of malpractice, and multiple other clarifications of right and wrong do not come from a cyclical attitude that every day repeats the day before. We do seek not only what is possible but also what is moral.

The following chapters discuss this biblical view of the human being in the world. God's Word informs us about creation and the fall and redemption of all creation in the demanding context of real life. Here the hunger and thirst of people, the burdens of an unfriendly nature, and the frequent tyranny of human history are understood not as masters of our fate but as limits to be stretched and evils to be corrected.

The poverty of so many in the human family is not due simply to unfavorable conditions of weather and resources. Such problems are unfair, often undeserved, and always unacceptable. But poverty results not only from the cruelty of many people to their neighbors but also from a poverty of ideas about life, work, and meaning. That poverty is not always alleviated by religion. Quite the contrary, it is often religion's logical and practical result.

"Religion," Sara said, "is not merely useless. Religion is dangerous."[1]

"Why consult the dead on behalf of the living?"[2]

---

1 Anthony Burgess, *The Kingdom of the Wicked* (London: Hutchinson, 1985), 282.
2 Isaiah 8:19.

I

Water and Worldviews

We had driven at high speed all day in Al's Toyota, going east of Nairobi. At first the road was level and took us through very pleasant land with villages, plenty of trees, and marvelous contrasts of light brown earth with dark green forests and blue sky. The good road ended behind Thika. As we gradually descended toward Kitui District, dirt and dust began to enter through the holes for the gearshift and the pedals on the floor. I was surprised that he would drive the relatively new car with so little care.

Al had lived in Africa for many years and had always driven at this speed. His theory was that you can either go slowly and feel every pothole in the road or fly over them at fifty miles an hour. Great baobab trees gave us shade from time to time. Sections of tree trunks hung in them, hollowed out to serve as hives for honeybees. By a creek, bricks were being made and baked in the hot sun. People greeted us as we flew past them. Children played in doorways. As women carried firewood on their heads or made their way to the water holes, their elegant steps stirred a slight breeze in which their brightly colored clothes waved. When the trees eventually receded to line only the riverbeds, we could see men watching their cattle and goats the way children watch their pennies roll when their piggy banks are opened. The herd is the roving investment of a family. Soon enormous reddish and brown monoliths rose out of the drier ground. We reached Muru in the late afternoon.

We were greeted warmly by the staff of the small hospital, built at one end of a giant granite rock. We could see that the Dutch doctor in charge was giving her life for the health of all the villagers in the area. Two couples welcomed us with tea in the mission station two miles away on the other side of the same rock, shaped like an elephant's back. Its appearance reminded me of Ayers Rock in central Australia. I was surprised to find three large steel tanks next to the hospital. During the two rainy seasons, typical in East Africa, a low wall forming the letter *Y* channeled whatever water ran off that part of the smooth mountain into a little aqueduct. This would fill the cisterns with rainwater. More than 450,000 gallons of water are stored in this way two seasons a year. It is enough for the needs of the hospital, its daily patients, and their families for the six months between the rainy seasons.

Water—and with it, life—is less stable in the village. The young principal in his school at the foot of the mountain described the lives of his students and the difficulties in their education, health care, and supervision. Although children need continuity for their education and medical supervision, a great migration regularly takes place during the drier seasons. When the rain ceases, the animals follow the receding river to continue grazing. The adults follow their animals; the children follow their parents. The school gradually empties. Classes start with 450 pupils and dwindle between two seasons each year to fewer than a hundred.

Education is dictated here by the schedule of nature's provisions. Health care is difficult, since little continuity for comparative checkups is guaranteed. Stability is impossible when nature dictates the patterns of human life. I pointed to the water tanks, which had been installed decades ago here and at other places when European influence was more than colonialism. The principal said that this was a wonderful and interesting way of dealing with the hardship of unsteady water supplies, but he also saw it as very Western and not the way indigenous people had chosen to live. In fact, no one in the village had used any of the remaining surface of the rock, about 2.5 miles in circumference, to tap rainwater in one way or another before it flowed to the ground. It seeped into the parched soil unused and was quickly gone instead of being stored in a place for use by the villagers during the long dry seasons.

I suggested very gently that more than something Western was being exhibited here. The determination and effort to redirect and to collect the water are the expressions of a different way of seeing nature, people, and life itself. It is not Western, but the fruit of a different set of ideas, which produced much of the so-called West in the first place. Behind the material possibilities created by means of simple tools and available resources lies a view of the world that differs from the traditionalism of African religions and the fatalism of most other religions. Just as traditions and fatalism shape societies and individual behavior, the worldview given in the Bible also creates a particular outlook and practice.

According to the Bible, the human being is the crown of God's creation. Human beings are children of God and, therefore, should not see themselves as merely helpless victims of natural circumstances. Nature did not bear them. Nor is nature the revelation of God. God is not found in nature; he is outside of it, for nature is his creation.

In its present state nature bears witness not only to God but also to the effects of Adam's fall. It bears witness to God's power, but no longer to his moral character. Nature is in need of being studied, evaluated, and possibly judged and changed on the basis of God's instructions in his Word. The Bible tells us that nature is now also fallen, often hostile, and quite difficult to live with.

Nature must be analyzed for correction wherever it crushes human life and then possibly be changed. After the fall of Adam and Eve, God told the first people that thorns and thistles must be plowed under to make room for human existence, for food, and for a more stable life (Genesis 3). The land must be cultivated, or we could say that nature must be "incultured." The damaged wilderness must be made habitable; weeds must be taken away from places where food needs to grow to feed human beings.

The difference between the two approaches on display in Muru does not lie in know-how. Nor is there an essential difference of material resources. The difference is, in fact, a display of profoundly different views of the value of life, that is, different views of human beings in the midst of the real world, in the tragic or wounded experience of life. One approach leads to skills and discoveries, and the other leads to fatalism. It is not a Western model in opposition to others, but the innovative model became associated with the West during the course of history in Africa and around the world.

The teachings of the Bible lead troubled or questioning people to initiate alternative approaches in dealing with the results of nature's normal annual patterns. In Muru, nature's patterns prolong the pain and suffering of the village. The people need water, yet nature, geography, physics, and wider circumstances often do not provide it. Because nature has no compassion, humans must care and recognize that the pain in real life needs correction and not acquiescence, tolerance, or denial.

The God of the Bible is Lord and Master over what occurs in our daily experience. He does not only observe. He also intervenes frequently and encourages new evaluations, moral judgment, and interference against whatever is broken in a fallen world.

The contrast illustrated in Muru is not simply between Western and indigenous ways of doing things, but between different views of the world in which we live. The one looks at life from the perspective the Bible gives about God and human beings, about life and death, about a fallen rather than a normal reality. The other perspective assumes that nature is the final authority. It is the pagan outlook in the sense that *pagus* (Latin for "land," "region," "nature") is the final underlying determinant.

Whether we receive information about all of life from God through the Bible or from taking nature and ancestral patterns as a cue makes a dramatic difference in the lives of people as well as their natural environments. God and human beings add to the shape of reality a moral dimension that is absent when impersonal nature, the flow of history, and the cold study of facts are the final horizon. Passion, concern, and justice are expressions of personality. They are not found in the floods of rain or the parched soil under the African sun. No amount of admiration for both the real beauty of the land and the devotion of people to their families must make us blind to the tragic results of a fatalistic worldview that brings unnecessary suffering to anyone in the human family.

A biblical worldview demands that we recognize the shape of the real world in its normality and judge it in its fallen and imperfect present condition as abnormal. It is what it is, but it should not always be that way. The fall of Adam broke the harmony with the good Creator. All reality afterward was damaged and no longer reflects in any part the full goodness and glory of the Creator. Consequently, the Bible admonishes us to make an effort to change and repair a broken creation. It calls us to work against natural conditions. The mandate to have dominion over creation before the fall of Adam is expanded in the mandate to stop the spread of thorns and thistles after the fall, for the sake of life. Jesus himself came to defeat sin in all its manifestations, including death itself. He healed the sick, denounced bondage of the human mind, corrected false perceptions, and fed the hungry. He encourages better government and demands love that includes even enemies, in the hope of convincing them of their fallacies.

With this perspective, Jews and Christians travel far, study hard, and expose themselves to criticism in pursuit of helping others by delivering them from the burdens of natural disasters and the prisons of man-made erroneous beliefs (though they may claim to be revealed!). There is love and compassion coupled with hard work and courage to denounce evil and fight death in any of its ugly faces. What is specifically Christian about such activity is not a mere feeling of love and sharing, but the expression of love in a world of facts. It involves substantial material relief and better-reasoned explanations of the problems. A biblical approach distinguishes and acknowledges the pain and then brings specific relief to underscore a distinctive way of thinking, living, and acting.

Often the material relief itself—the surplus of food, time, and funds—is available as the result of a more realistic mindset and belief founded on a biblical view of reality that is always demanded and confirmed by reality itself. More often the surplus exists from work, effort, and responsibility than from theft or mere geographical luck.

With that mindset we are also responsible to examine ourselves from time to time. We do not want to do things out of habit without renewed conviction or without sensitivity. The perversity of human nature and the role of being teachers/professionals can keep us from the needed examination of what should be done. We may settle back in the belief that we already do the right things and that we already know enough. Reflection and skill, ideas and material resources constitute the intervention mentality. Stepping in is essential if human suffering is to be reduced, and it can be reduced only when both the material need and the intellectual/moral origins of the problems are addressed.

Jesus never performed a miracle or never confronted the evil of his own day without a "sermon" explaining the authority with which he materially objected to the evil of sickness, false teaching, or hunger. His miracles never were freak events of some gratuitous grace. He always presented a spiritual/intellectual context for the power of God in word and deed.

A review and further study of the real world and the content of our calling as Christians should enlighten us in at least two areas. We must see the material and natural problems and limitations, and we must recognize the social, political, and religious context of needy people. Both the material limits and the moral/cultural limits need to be overcome for effective and lasting help. Without the biblical order and its information about all areas of life, we will largely fail in our efforts to effect change. The hearts and minds of people must be addressed, informed, nourished, and corrected where necessary.

Without this component we function as agents wishing for social change but without the tools to affect the world of ideas, thoughts, and choices. We will not accomplish a lasting and sustained change if we are unwilling to interact with (and most likely to gently and persistently interfere with) those religious, social, and cultural ideas that stand in the way of personal, economic, social, and political development.

We may be driven to lend a hand by personal desire, by moral outrage, by a sense of guilt and frustration, by a spirit of revenge, or by a longing to demonstrate unity in the human family. A concern for material fairness or even equality seeks to diminish the obvious differences that exist between individuals and cultures around the world. We recognize a diversity of historical, cultural values and treasure the idea of material equality for the well-being of hurting people. But we dare not neglect that other, more spiritual and intellectual, hierarchy of values that is made up of wise or foolish ideas about all of life. These have their origin in people's worldviews and their religious orientations. They find expression in their broad cultural choices and detailed practices.

Ideas have consequences. What we believe about life and death, man and woman and beast, nature and culture, and temporary and permanent things will shape the way we order priorities and definitions. Where there is little concern for precise measurements in relation to life in the real world, we will also find little ability to provide for sustenance, for law, and for steady and trusting relationships among people. Where life's experiences are seen as the result of invisible forces or predetermined events, we will find little emphasis on the need to acquire skills and to take personal responsibility. A resigned attitude to the vagaries of life does not foster initiative. If nature, history, or the gods have placed a person into inevitable circumstances, there is little allowance or incentive for freedom, courage, or resistance.

A Christian motivation alone is not enough to engage in development work abroad, to prepare a new generation for the job market and civic responsibility, or to address social problems in our own societies. There are, of course, passages in the Bible calling for genuine compassion. The story of the Good Samaritan teaches us that all people are our neighbor. In emergencies, help is needed immediately without any questions asked or reservations held.

However, the Bible's record is more than a series of motivational morality stories. It is also a historical and intellectual witness to people and their ideas, for better or worse. It gives us a broader and more realistic understanding of the power of true and false ideas as well as the results of different faiths in the context of good and bad kings, fair and unfair judges, and wise and foolish human choices. The history of the Bible is the story of human actions and God's actions in the form of instruction, warning and judgment, and grace and forgiveness. It is a story of men and women always close to the edge of the abyss, to the border of disintegration and chaos. Moral anarchy is threatening to erupt at any moment.

The Bible includes the stories of those who went over the cliff into spiritual and material poverty. Some lived in Babel, others in Babylonian captivity. Later we find some in Corinth and in Jerusalem. And, of course, during all times, there have been the children of Cain who turn their backs on God in anger and then kill their brothers.

Christian work in society has always been characterized by a dedicated effort to stand against catastrophe and injustice. However, remedial help is but one side of our concern. The other side is the work against the causes of poverty. Although material needs cry the loudest for help, the poor ideas that produced the wounds and cries in the first place need also to be addressed.

Adam and Eve spoiled the good creation of God by believing something different about the world from what God had told them. Their idea about life was no longer nurtured by information from the Creator. They believed in a different world, one in which they could disregard God's word and instead become, in their own eyes, like God. They ate the forbidden fruit after believing the false promise of Satan, who was from then on well designated as the father of lies.

The remainder of the Bible reports with colorful illustrations the reality of the kind of things we are all too familiar with throughout human history. Either people believe what is true to the real world or they believe a lie. Either they dream about the impossible (whether an ideal, the desirable, or the worst) or they seek to figure out what is true from the study of nature, of people, and of revelation. Whatever they conclude will influence their decisions. And choices always have consequences.

Water and Worldviews

The Bible confronts us with a history of good and bad human choices between God and Baal, between God's Word and human counsel, and between finding individual meaning in life and simply submitting to resignation, to fate, to spirits, to majorities, or even to common views. The people of God in the Bible are not any different from us. The record of people in the context of all humankind mirrors us well. On behalf of the living, people either consult the dead or inquire of God, the Creator (Isaiah 8:19).

At all times individuals are making wise or foolish choices that affect the world around them. They make history and set the stage for the next generation. There is no going back to do it differently. This is the privilege and the price of significance.

Abraham chose to love God and to believe him when God promised a son through whom the Messiah would come to all people (Genesis 12:1–3; 15:4). Abraham had lived among the idolatrous people in Ur (Acts 7:2–4). They believed in gods of nature and of heavenly bodies, the moon and stars, while Abraham believed in Jehovah. He believed what he knew to be true even against the collective religious convictions of, first, the people of Ur and, later, his new neighbors in Canaan.

When he split with Lot over where to live because of the crowded pasture land (Genesis 13), Lot chose to join the cities with pagan rulers while Abraham continued his distinct life and faith. He was noticed for his different views and practices by King Abimelech (Genesis 21:22–34). Abraham and Isaac believed something very different from the nations living in Canaan about God and their relationship to God and life (Genesis 22). The latter practiced human sacrifice. They gave of their best and killed their own children, hoping to maintain their comfort and to save their own skins; Abraham did not.

The difference came down to two visions of God. Abraham and the Canaanites had different views on who God is, how humans relate to God, and, consequently, how to understand human existence. Abraham knew and worshiped Jehovah. The Canaanites tried to appease and model Baal. Jehovah is a person, the creator of life, and a moral being in heaven. Baal was the Canaanite deity thought to be behind the functioning of nature, its mysteries, its tragedies, its indifference, and in short—its impersonality.

Abraham understood that he was in relationship with a person who made promises (Genesis 15 and 17), who could be argued with (Genesis 18), and who explained the tragedy of life in terms of the consequence of human sin. Abraham had hope because God would provide the necessary sacrifice of appeasement (Genesis 22:8). Abraham and the boy would descend from the mountain together (22:5). There was yet a promise of God outstanding, so the whole experience around the sacrifice of Isaac would not end in the death of this child of promise. Through Isaac would come the blessing of all nations.

The Canaanites saw the origin of all existence as impersonal. Deities existed behind the events of life and needed to be encouraged, manipulated, and restrained. Meaning and models for human activities were sought in the universal of nature and fertility and the normal cycles of what is largely a cruel existence: birth and death in regular sequence. The cues for life were hidden behind what happens in nature. People must emulate nature and, thereby, show approval, submission, and humble participation.

A portion of the Abrahamic covenant with and from God was the promise of land (Genesis 12:7). There is a time and space dimension to God's actions and to human existence. Salvation is not something in a person's mind, but in history. The later warning about moving boundary stones (Deuteronomy 19:14) was anticipated in Abraham's insistence on purchasing Sarah's tomb, rather than using a site donated by the Hittites. Although he remained a sojourner in Canaan while waiting for the fulfillment of the promise about the land (Genesis 15:2), Abraham wanted a little piece of that land for Sarah's burial (Genesis 23). He exercised dominion over nature, over the opinion of others, and over the temptation to join them in their wrong views.

Abraham is praised in Scripture for his independence from natural, cultural, and social dictates. He found the strength for this in the realization that God's Word was completely trustworthy. God, not creation, was Abraham's universal principle. He believed and acted accordingly. He dug wells to nourish his flock and became wealthy. He changed the course of water because he saw himself as a child of God, not of natural settings. His covenant was with God, not with nature or the world around him. "Abraham believed God, and it was credited to him as righteousness" (Romans 4:3). He is praised in the list of faithful people (Hebrews 11:8–10) because he made his home in the Promised Land, "a place he would later receive as his inheritance" and where he waited for a city "whose . . . builder is God."

More basic than a different historical experience is the difference in attitude toward historical events. Abraham saw the world differently than his neighbors. A good God created it. Need, suffering, and frustrations were the result of sin, not an original part of creation or part of a creative process that is always, at the same time, destructive as well. Therefore, Abraham dared to change the face of reality. He did not accept the dictates of nature but lived by the Word of God alone. That word gave him his cues.

Adam had been given the mandate to rule over creation. He had been called to work by the sweat of his brow after the fall when nature became abnormal. Like Adam, believers turned to God for instruction and moral orientation. The world around them could not provide that because it was impersonal and would always be a poor, if not devastating, model for human life.

Pursuant to this insight, Abraham and his son Isaac dug wells.[1] They needed water for their families and their herds. Since nature did not sufficiently provide it, water had to be discovered and accessed by creative work. The Hebrews had the freedom to do this because they did not view nature as the final authority over their existence. Water was a necessary resource hidden underground, and it could be used to solve a problem. Believing God's Word caused the Hebrews to value life. Therefore, creative labor to sustain life and to diminish recognized problems was justified and encouraged.

The accounts of Abraham and Isaac digging wells to access the water are more than stories about water rights. They are stories against a background of different worldviews. We find here more than the frequent troubles over water sources in nomadic cultures, where the stronger will drive away the weaker unless a system of distribution is in place. The context itself suggests a deeper contrast. It relates to different concepts of life, of God, of property, of land, and of personal responsibilities.

The accounts are framed by the juxtaposition of two worldviews. Basically, it is a question of whether a person believes in Jehovah or Baal; in other words, the question is whether there is a God who created nature or whether God is there in nature. Is God's word *the* source of wisdom and

---

1   Genesis 26.

responsibility, or are they sourced in the natural workings of the world we live in? The first conclusion leads to activity, imagination, creativity, and responsibility. The second leads to submission, blind obedience, and fatalism resulting in continued suffering. The first requires a moral decision about the world we live in after the fall. The second (resignation) makes us accomplices of a painful and often immoral situation.

The God of Abraham is a personal God. He thinks, feels, and acts. He speaks and encourages; he clarifies and answers. He has passions and emotions of love and grief. He has made a covenant with a human, whom he addressed as a partner. That treaty established obligations for Abraham and for God. God can be argued with, and his words explain and help us understand such situations as death, suffering, and natural disasters. We are encouraged that Moses, Jeremiah, Job, and even Jesus argued with God, because life is at present not normal, moral, or just.

And God explains himself in reference to a spoiled creation of which he is not the author. Yet he does not withdraw from it. Instead, he got busy after his day of rest to accomplish a new task—to restore creation on the eighth day, the day also of the resurrection. He ran after Adam and gave instructions on how to limit the damage of the fall, how to resist death with another generation of children, and how to continue in hope of the salvation that would come in the future through a woman's child, the promised Messiah.

Abraham and his children still make the desert bloom, dig wells, and struggle for righteousness while the Canaanites and their descendants must bow to the normal circumstances of a hard life, following their pagan or earth-based religions. They obey their masters, their fate, and their condition while Christians and Jews question, critique, and always doubt the finality of the present.

God created an unfinished world that gives room for people to have dominion instead of being victims in an accomplished and closed situation. Christians stand against death and for life and set law against chaos, water against drought, and children against the body's return to dust at death. Their ideas, drawn from God's word, inform both actions and priorities. Christians pursue what *could be* with creative energy and what *ought to be* with moral conviction. Knowing merely the way things already are in nature gives no moral courage to seek what ought to be. Biblical ideas come from heaven, not from earth, and their consequent actions are motivated not from impersonal science, but from a creation mandate, from moral conviction, and from effective passion.

Our understanding—trained, informed, corrected, and encouraged from God's word—propels individuals into the arena of life. Rather than submitting to the collective, to traditions, and to some notion of permanence seen in the cycles of nature, Christians make decisions and take initiative individually in obedience to the God who also acts. He came running after Adam, calling out, "Where are you?" He sent prophets, came to lunch with Abraham, and sent his Son to die for sin and to be raised as the first of many for the righting of God's creation.

In the biblical perspective, the greatest resource for people is the knowledge of a different and particular God. His existence and words challenge us to a more critical and creative existence. The compassion to help others, the mandate to relieve suffering, the obligation to serve the state whenever it limits evil are only thinkable after we have rejected an attitude of resignation or blind submission to normality. These are moral concerns. And morality exists only if God himself is moral and accountable, as presented in the Bible.

In the narrative of the stopped-up wells (Genesis 26:12–18), the Canaanites were envious of Isaac's success. But rather than learning from the God of Isaac, they destroyed the beneficial results of the Hebrew worldview. The Canaanites were resentful and unwilling to learn. They were so caught in their religion that even the evidence of a beneficial alternative did not free them to discover the God of the Bible. Not having the ideas in their religion, they destroyed what they could have used. They filled up the wells and, thereby, continued their own poverty. They were prisoners of their religion and customs and remained ignorant of the freedom of the children of God. Rather than learning critically with benefit for all, they resented that others had what they did not have. They preferred maintaining a community of poverty in the security of traditions and the sorrowful marriage of resentment and suspicion.

Their culture was fundamentally suffering from a poverty of ideas. This resulted in a poverty of personality that, in turn, had consequences in their economic and social life. They had their religion, but reality was not allowed to challenge it. They were rich in a faith that made them poor in reason, personal honesty, and moral quality. They saw the light but were afraid to walk in it. They were prisoners of their inhuman religions, their indigenous habits, and their traditions.

People like this today would still rather die in their ways than become free to live. They might call it the will of god or of Allah, the way of the ancients, traditions, or fate. They might advocate it as patriotism, local traditions, and collective interest. But they never question the morality of a broken world. And with that they deny the greatest resource: their own worth as persons who are children of God, not of an impersonal nature. Their religions, centering on an impersonal notion of nature and its rules, are the greatest hindrance to their personhood.

The specifically Christian component about biblical compassion toward those in need involves more than generous aid in relief and development, education and statecraft, and business and social involvement. It also requires careful analysis of those religious, intellectual, social, political, and cultural ideas that war against the human being. These concepts need to be challenged to give greater honor to human beings, for we are each too different in our personhoods to have emerged from impersonal nature. Yet many will consider nature as final, or as god, with the result that the human person is always the victim of nature's impersonal whims. Personality cannot result from impersonality. Persons have been made individually in the image of Jehovah.

Faulty and inhuman views with such extensive consequences need to be corrected, refuted, and unmasked. Giving material relief alone is much like giving a Band-Aid. It only protects the superficial wound. But where suffering, poverty, and death are the results of flawed ideas about life, the task demands a dedicated, careful surgery for getting to the infection. We do not just hold the hands of those in misery. We catch the water for their thirst and filter it to be used several times over. We dig wells and build cisterns for freedom from the daily battle against drought due to irregular rainy seasons.

But the victims also need to change their views about God, life, and work to create in a lasting way for themselves the sense, the beauty, and the effectiveness of such efforts.

God sent prophets and Jesus Christ to win the battle against the lies and erroneous views that deceived Adam, Eve, and all their children. We are sent to declare the same understanding to those who suffer because of the lies they embraced when they chose to follow inhuman religions and ideologies.

2
Bread, Fish, and a Better Focus

When Stalin's army started the return offensive to drive back the Germans from White Russia and the Ukraine in 1943, a community of German-speaking Mennonites was caught between them. They feared Stalin's anger against all Germans. He had, after all, driven out most Volga Germans in forced marches from the southern regions to the Altai Mountains in Kazakhstan, to Omsk and Tomsk in Siberia, and to Vorkuta, north of the polar circle. It was not good to have roots in the German language and culture anywhere in Russia in those days.

The Mennonites did not want to go to Nazi Germany, however. A door opened for them to immigrate to Paraguay, which welcomed all Germans. They were given land and settled in the dry, hilly, and shrub-covered Chaco area. For centuries the area had been very thinly populated. Natives lived there in the regular sequence of experiences that follows the seasons of the year and the birth-to-death cycle of human life. They made a bare living, the harshness of the land being a constant restraint on their possibilities and their hopes.

The Mennonites arrived as a group of people with a very different worldview. Their social order, their attitudes toward work and leisure, and their devotion to their families and to their religion were deliberate and defined. They studied their Bibles, which spoke to them of the high calling of being God's children with a purposeful life. They settled in a new freedom, building houses and shops, schools and churches, and staking out fields and carving roads in much the same way they had done earlier in Russia. They worked hard and with a purpose, passing on skills from fathers to sons and from mothers to daughters. Each one had an appreciated place in the community, and they depended on each other. They were skilled and motivated, and they had a worldview that valued life.

Over the next forty years, the community grew prosperous, though without any great luxury. Children went to school and learned new trades. They made the land bear fruit and attempted to settle conflicts peacefully. With determined efforts they gave the wilderness a more cultured shape. They developed a thriving dairy industry.

On the two banks of the river stood the two different cultures, each one the result of its ideas and nurturing efforts. The natives continued in their fear, their exposure, and their fatalism to barely make a living for those strong enough to survive. With much organization, but without much intellectual and spiritual motivation to change the greater force of nature's patterns, they let nature's indifference roll over them and leave them flat.

By contrast, the Mennonites had brought with them a different view of life, of work, of men and women. They shaped nature to serve them, without exploiting it harshly in return. Their view was one of faithfulness to the God of the Bible, not of faithfulness to the surrounding natural and cultural patterns. What had separated them from both Stalin and Hitler had also made them distinct from the indigenous group of natives who had never heard about the truth of Christianity concerning all of life.

The story of the Mennonite effort and success illustrates, in another geographical area, the power of ideas in the lives of people. What we think about ourselves, the world we live in, and the purpose of life for the individual and that individual's family will shape our actions. *Ideas Have Consequences* is the title of Richard Weaver's early book. This title states one of the central truths about human society. It should be considered whenever we set out to deal honestly with human tragedy, with suffering, and with other kinds of need. It should constrain us to review earlier ideas and to change them, when painful consequences reveal flaws, including bondage to folksy or religious traditions.

We are called to compassion toward those who are in need. However, too often our compassion is developed from a materialist mindset alone. Need is defined in terms of having or not having material resources. We easily reduce compassion to the distribution of things instead of elevating the communication and explanation of better ideas, since we rarely understand the social and economic value of good ideas. Ideas are not measurable, while things can be quantified, amounts compared, and inequalities complained about and corrected.

The Christian life and its social vision call for compassion. Jesus taught compassion in a number of incidents and expressed statements. The stories of the miracles of healing and the feeding of the multitude are some of the numerous examples in the Bible. These narratives are in the broad context of the Bible's admonition to help those in need. We live in a fallen world in which the effects of sin should be reduced by acts of justice and mercy. The New Testament teachings on compassion continue the Old Testament tradition of providing for widows and orphans. Both give concrete expression to the character of God, who immediately ran after Adam to promise and command practical steps that would diminish the consequences of believing a lie.

Compassion extends to the poor within our gates and even to the aliens among us. Acts of mercy should be deliberate and not left to random decisions. Benevolence counters the suffering and poverty in which many people live without hope of ever escaping their inhuman conditions.

Christian appeals for justice come from sensitivity to unfair situations. Neither dishonest distribution nor overconsumption of resources is ultimately acceptable. We are deeply troubled by both waste and lack. Injustice is unacceptable and is the source of much grief. While so much can be accomplished through human effort, the benefits are not available to all in need.

Sensitivity to human sin makes us aware of the adverse effects of selfish decisions. Poor choices include certain aspects of colonialism and widespread laziness, corruption, and lack of accountability. We must also include failure to address pagan religious views and life patterns in societies, which gnaw away at the possibility of civilized human existence. The recognition of evil aspects of colonialism provides an easy and obvious explanation for the tragic human conditions in some parts of the world. Far more difficult and complex is the recognition of the indigenous evil of people, which results from their worldview. At times, the colonizers came not to import or create new evil but to diminish already existing evil with compassionate intentions. The creation of schools, hospitals, and churches were not efforts to subdue, but to liberate people caught in the prison of inhuman habits and unjustified fears.

In order to meet obvious needs, much of the public concern for the poor is focused on a better and more equitable system of resource distribution. We are admonished to equitably share our abundance with many. Often Christians have adopted this view without any further consideration, such as the many different ways wealth is created. The appeal to our consciences seeks a remedy to inequality and unfairness. From a concern for tangible results, a demonstration of a more spiritual, less materialist, attitude is expected. The story of the Good Samaritan in Luke's Gospel is read to illustrate this sharing obligation. We are reminded to love those in need and to share with them our material and personal wealth. We should lay up treasure in heaven and resist greed. Christ's warning about trusting in external things and Paul's admonition against the love of money are also drawn on.

Most admonitions to help those in need are couched in terms of guilt. We are guilty because of our lifestyle, our consumption. Our failure to do more is seen as the cause of suffering and death around the world. A relation is suggested between the plenty in our hands and the empty hands of others. What we consume is missing elsewhere. The general assumption is that their need is due to our greed.

Yet the Bible presents more than a moral proposition; it also presents an economic and a historical perspective, which must be considered as well. Unless this is done, a zero-sum assumption exists. This assumption is that the amount of available resources is permanently fixed, neither increasing nor decreasing. Resources cannot be added by additional effort and discovery. The total benefit to all involved, for every combination of strategies, always equals zero (i.e., a person benefits only at the expense of others, the amount lacking for some equals the amount of abundance for others). Abundance or waste on one side will result in lack and need on the other, so that putting the two together equals zero.

A simple version was expressed in my mother's admonition against waste: "Finish what is on your plate. People in China would be happy to get what you have left on your plate!" This assumed that what I had, they lacked, in part, because it was still on my plate. Of course, I then tried to do what my mother told me to do. That would diminish her criticism, and it would also remove my guilt for starving the Chinese. Should I have sent it to them instead of eating it? I remember, in fact, once responding, "Then take it and send it to them from me!"

This concern, moral though it sounds, primarily focuses on distribution, while the questions concerning production of resources—those dealing with economics and history—are not usually reviewed. Generally, the fault is seen to lie in unequal access to the world's limited goods. Often left out of the discussion are such pivotal issues as how the worldviews of the people in need have affected the situation—what ideas are held about God, humans and work, and the use of time, and how any of these affects production of resources.

Our consideration here is not primarily economic or historical, but instead touches on worldviews. Much evil was practiced under colonial rule in the past. At the same time, the present reality of people dying because of hunger is largely not the result of colonialism but of present mismanagement, inhumanity, false religious views, and inhibiting social customs. In short, the tragedy of human sin and suffering is daily a repeated experience more than an inherited burden. It did not begin or end with colonialism, the West, or the white male.

It is remarkable that only the context of Jewish and Christian thought and tradition has ever given rise to moral objection where unjust human suffering is perceived, whether concerning its own people or the alien at the gate. There is no self-criticism in Islam, for it can never be wrong in its own eyes. There is none found in Buddhism, since its highest goal is the elimination of critical awareness in a state of enlightenment. The concern for human rights is essentially a biblical concern, for according to the Bible each person has rights given by the Creator, who made people and not just things. Universal human rights do not exist in Marxist societies, neither in Islamic, Buddhist, or Hindu culture, much less in traditional African tribes and nations.

Jesus Christ is for many the model of a man of compassion. In his teaching and practice he reached out to those in need and healed them. He stood against the closed assumptions of those in authority. He warned of judgment for those who neglected to provide for the poor. The Bible says that he is the express image of the eternal God in bodily form (Hebrews 1:3), the exact representation of God's being. We need to see here how his teaching sheds light on the discussion of what is the Christian view of relief, development, and social responsibilities at home and around the world.

The record of the feeding of the five thousand is found in all four Gospels. People followed Jesus and became, of course, hungry as they listened to him for a whole day in the wilderness and far from a town. He gave them bread and fish miraculously by multiplying what someone had brought for himself. When the people wanted to follow him for more food and drink the next day, Jesus pushed them away and spoke to them about a greater need that he came to meet. He sent the disciples across the lake and withdrew into the mountains.

Jesus did not start a social program centered on communal feeding of the poor. His words against their expectations of another free lunch even shook the people so much that a vast majority deserted him at that time. "You do not want to leave too, do you?" he asked the disciples (John 6:67). Their response is startling: "To whom shall we go? You have the words of eternal life" (v. 68). This is not a record of their hope for a more charitable distribution of food in the future on the basis of the one-time example just experienced. They understood that all of life requires God's word, not just food. That information of words concerning life would enable them to create food and to trade, for it would give them an explanation large enough to pursue life with meaning and in expectation of significant results in the social and economic realms.

The feeding of the five thousand did not start a movement. By contrast, there was a declining interest. The large crowd at the beginning decreased to become the small number of disciples who remained. The hope for having physical needs met in a new way after the miraculous first time was disappointed when Jesus taught that the true bread is to believe him and his word. The crowd that had followed Christ into the mountains deserted him. What they may easily have perceived as a new social program ended in spoiled hope. They began to see that bread for the stomach is only a temporary sign, indicative of the need for the true bread from heaven for the soul. The true bread is to believe what is spoken from the mouth of God.

The crowd had hoped for a renewed granting of manna from heaven. In the time of Moses during the wilderness wanderings, it had been the nation's daily provision. The crowd envisioned its material needs being met from heaven again. They forgot that even the manna in the Old Testament had been given by God to demonstrate his people's need to depend on his Word (Deuteronomy 8:3–9) and to obey it in all areas. That bread had fed the people for a while, but then they died in the wilderness through disobedience. Jesus repeated what the Old Testament taught. Lasting help comes only from believing God's Word and bringing it to life in practical application, thought forms, and habits.

The crowd had wanted to make Jesus king by force (John 6:15). They saw Jesus as a grand provider without a budget problem! But he taught them that God wanted to reign in their hearts and minds and instruct them about all of life. That would be the way to create food and all other things for life in a manner that no social program or distribution system could provide. It would answer basic questions of how people are different from animals. It would address questions of purpose and how to deal with a damaged world, rather than assuming that the daily mix of painful and good experiences is normal. It would raise all kinds of questions to which God's Word and human activity would provide answers not found in nature. Creation of resources is as much a concern for God and human beings as the distribution, which lasts only as long as existing resources are available. New resources need to be continually created.

When we look at the feeding episode (the crowd that

followed and wanted more and its desire to have a king who would feed it), we are reminded of Frederic Engels' program that people need bread, not ideas. With Marx, the revolution promised to provide not only bread but also cake for all. But the Bible's directive is the opposite, as found in Jesus' words. People need bread in the immediate emergency. But for lasting provisions in the hardships of life, they need ideas and living words about the truth of the universe. They need answers to the pressing questions of life. They need corrected insight about the place of men and women in history and creation. Faulty views have created death, poverty, and political, social, and religious confusion around the world; whereas views informed by the Bible have given food, security, and freedom and have made lives more humane. Biblical concepts have also made us more sensitive and critical about our place in life. Before, these results were lacking, or good ideas were used for only selfish ends.

There are many faulty systems of distribution, from human will and by whim of nature or geography. They all need to be corrected. Yet the real poverty lies in a faulty set of ideas about the world we live in. These flawed ideas relate to the production of resources, to the knowledge of God, and to the dignity of human beings made in the image of God.

The Bible brings people up short. It forces them to examine life's basic questions that do not focus primarily on a concern for bread or cake—though without food people

Bread, Fish, and a Better Focus

cannot even ask the questions. But once fed, a person must ask the permanent and central questions: Is there a God around anywhere? Who is he? Why is the world a mess? What kind of a world does this God identify with? What does he do about the present situation? What does he mandate and empower me to do in my social, political, and natural situation? What ideas have contributed to the painful life I experience?

These are fundamental questions. Is there a creator, or is my world the result of chance in an impersonal world? Are we a part of and exposed to nature, to fate, participating in mere being? If there is a creator, is he moral? How can he be moral in a world like ours? Has this world been around forever? Will it continue in this wasteful way? Is reality merely an illusion of the mind, or are there realities like death, suffering, and hunger? If God exists, what is he doing about our pain, our tears, and our tragedy?

How do I explain evil? Have I contributed to it by my choices? Do I resist or accept what happens around me in nature and culture? Am I like Job or one of his friends? Does reality trouble me enough to seek alternatives? Do I accept everything as inevitable, the will of my religion's god, or do I suffer without recourse under the cycles of occult normality?

These are the deeper issues that need to be addressed. Providing only food and shelter from the outside contributes to the continuation of a sick life, a hideous perversion, and a prolonging of death. Such efforts, without involving efforts to bring about cultural change as well, only make human suffering seem normal and acceptable. Band-Aids do not heal the underlying infection, and temporary relief does not address the underlying problems.

Important questions like these find no acceptable answers outside of the Bible. In most religions around the world, the individual is told to stop asking questions rather than receiving realistic answers. People are taught that they are the problem when they ask questions and in this way show their curiosity, their uniqueness, and their doubts. Religions provide a way to merge people with the universal (what has always been and is most powerful) and then abandon them there without any answers. People are merged into a larger reality at the expense of their own significance. They are part of a community born from traditions, collective practices, and silenced minds. Ceasing to be an individual person in this way will also make the questions disappear. The answer is always that the individual is already contained *in* the answer, swallowed up in it and submitting to it.

You may remember V. S. Naipaul's description of the common experiences of the Hindu (*An Area of Darkness*, 2002; see also *India: A Wounded Civilization*, 2003). Naipaul explains why that religion has not been able to help intellectually or materially: Man is born surrounded by much mud. Death is normal and ubiquitous. Man is lost in the cosmos as

Bread, Fish, and a Better Focus

an individual. He is called to abandon self by the acceptance of the inevitable. Complaint from a position of moral opposition is meaningless. Rejecting your karma and dharma only leads to greater sorrow in the next reincarnation.

To seek real change in your situation is impossible for three reasons. First, the individual is too small in the eternal cycle of being. Second, any objection to the present experience brings with it judgment and a worse experience in the next reincarnation. Third, nothing really new can be brought into the equation of being. Hinduism is a religiously justified system of present discrimination that rewards indifference about the present with a promise of a better life next time around.

Detachment from observed and experienced pain is also the highest achievement in Buddhism. Nirvana is reached when nothing will trouble you or shake your status of being part of a unified nothingness, because the categories of pain, sorrow, justice, life, and death are no more part of your awareness. All is One and you are All.

Similarly, in Islam all events are the expression of the will of Allah. Again, you are called to fit in and to accept the inevitable. You may not be able to understand this, but then who do you think you are in relation to the eternal, the whole, or a mysterious idea of God? You are called to join the community of believers and follow the rules and practices down to the smallest detail within the collective. Enjoyment of the aesthetic miracle of the Qur'an is the meaning of life. It involves no change, no questions, and no search for a just life.

These religious views lead to resignation, to a denial of human and real problems, and to a view of "again and again" so characteristic of paganism. There is really nothing that could challenge the status quo. Things have always been this way. They are necessarily this way. Perhaps there is a hidden meaning somewhere. In each case, any problem lies in your way of seeing life, in your perception.[1]

Problems only exist because you fail to detach yourself from your erroneous assumption that you can see problems. There are no real problems; they have no real existence of their own. They disappear when you change your way of thinking. You must bow and, against all evidence, call it good. You may even find a hidden beauty when you join the dance of "everything." You submit and become one with what is bigger and more permanent than you.

The immediate context of the story about the feeding of the five thousand gives us these same responses from people

---

[1] See Daniel Boorstin, *The Discoverers* (New York: Random House, 1983). "Mankind was preparing a new arsenal of thought, and escape from the prison of Again-and-Again," 16. "The Muslim world . . . continued to meet in Mecca. But there was no counterpart place of Again-and-Again, no accessible site of obligatory return for all Christians," 122. "The great religions of the West, seeking to escape from the animal world of Again-and-Again, found an opposite path . . . [to the religions of the East with their] help to merge the individual into the All, . . . dissolving the individual into an unchanging anonymous Absolute," 566.

in Jesus' day. There is a remarkable sequence in the passages as Matthew lines up events for our instruction. We find very typical human reactions in which we find ourselves reflected.

Jesus' neighbors in his hometown of Nazareth saw his wisdom and power. But, ultimately, they explained it all away by seeing Jesus only as the son of Joseph. They were offended. They liked him but did not see in him anything extraordinary. Life had always been predictable for them. They chose to see Jesus in terms of their normality (Matthew 13:57–58). The people in Nazareth would not follow him, discover new things, and then reject the normality of their broken lives.

Faced with life's tragedies, most people will respond with views that bow to and accept the inevitable. Thereby, they become less personal, for they would rather give up their moral reaction than face an unresolved problem. They begin to see their moral motions as a mistake, a matter of wishful thinking, but ultimately out of place, for persistent moral objections would leave life unresolved.

If they believed in the God of the Bible, however, that would not be a problem, because God will not be finished with history until the work of Christ is completed and righteousness is once again established. Yet most people would rather make peace now with everything, even when it involves abandoning their moral objections to what now seems normal. They make no attempt to find out how they might come to understand God's mind. Instead, they resign themselves to the again and again of history, to destiny. They may talk about the will of God and forget that all life now takes place in a fallen world.

Some others respond differently. They reject resignation, set themselves up, and, by an act of the will, make a life for themselves without further considerations. They will drink and be merry, for they know that tomorrow they will die. While the majority accepts impersonality, the few practice immorality. That response is illustrated with the events at the court of Herod, again in the context of the feeding (Matthew 14:1–12). Here a king who made up his own rules dealt with life's absurdity and unanswered questions in his own way. He created a mini-universe around his position, title, and power. His world was a world of power, pleasure, and perversion. When John the Baptist confronted him with God's law, Herod had John's head served up on a platter. Herod had been occupied with himself, ignorant of the larger picture, until John, the stranger, came with powerful words and admonitions to question Herod's assumed title to his brother's wife.

Herod feared John because of the authority with which he spoke and judged. Herod knew him as holy, righteous, and esteemed by the many people who had gone out from Jerusalem to listen to him talk in the wilderness about repentance. But John's message became too personal and immediate for Herod. John exposed the whole artificiality of Herod's fame and power. But because of the dinner guests and certain promises he had made to his daughter, Herod could not back down, and John was beheaded.

In that sequence of events, Jesus drew a crowd to interrupt the assumed normality in the lives of his fellow citizens from Nazareth and the normal immorality of Herod's court. Jesus invited people to a different festive meal. There would be no horror of a head on a platter. But there would also be no indifference to the suffering of people in a sinful world. Neither blind activism for show nor neglect of real needs would characterize Jesus' words and work.

Instead, his feeding the crowd would demonstrate the real and supernatural existence of God. This would be a meal in the tradition of the miracle during the wedding at Cana. It would anticipate the last supper before the crucifixion and then the marriage supper of the Lamb in the future—festive celebrations that stand in contrast to the resignation of Nazareth ("nothing is ever really new") and the horrors of Herod's courtly powers ("you can't really ever do anything about it"). It anticipates the promise in Isaiah 49:8–9: "In the time of [the Lord's] favor . . . they will feed beside the roads and find pasture on every barren hill."

We do not have details about what Jesus taught the people assembled outside of town. Some in the crowd must have been horrified by the events at Herod's court while others had been discouraged by the apathy of the people in Nazareth in the face of human need. What they heard attracted them. Their hope was a renewed presence of God, a healing of their situations. They wanted a different society, hoping to make Christ king. One who can stand so powerfully and act with authority against the normality of tragic human existence must become the leader. Had the Messiah come?

But Jesus did not fulfill the hope for a new political and social program. He provided bread and fish to illustrate the need to listen to God's Word about all of life. The physical food would meet only an emergency. It could not prevent death. It would be like a Band-Aid to cover the wounds. But what they needed was spiritual food, that is, information and power from God about all of life—the past, present meaning, and future hope. This spiritual food would also explain the meaning of work, life in a fallen world, and relationships framed and grounded in the knowledge that there is a living God who will not abandon his creation.

Our life is derived from the living God. He created us as people and to be people. He created history so that we would be historically significant. He created a real world to be worked in, to be shaped and reshaped—even if it would be by the sweat of our brows after the fall of Adam. God is the source of life, and we must now choose to live passionately, constructively, and deliberately as rational and creative beings. We are not surrounded by energy only. Matter does not give life or meaning. Chance or energy in any form is not the beginning. We are not like balls bouncing around in the many games of nature.

The true bread from heaven is not manna, for the people who ate manna later died. Jesus is the true bread from heaven (John 6:33), and with Jesus in the flesh we discover God in history. The true bread that gives life is found in who Jesus is and what he reveals about God, human beings, and history. Through him we discover the certainty of a God who speaks, acts, and loves. By what Jesus said and what he did, we have knowledge from God about what he had in mind when he made human beings. He desires us to be informed by his Word in order to live with understanding, discernment, and motivation. That Word not only informs us about spiritual things in a narrow, platonic sense but also informs us about the material world. Deuteronomy 8 tells us how through the Word of God we know about salvation (v. 3) and rocks of iron and "where . . . you can dig copper out of the hills" (v. 9). God's Word concerns itself with both body and soul, the whole person created in God's image.

Words from God are spirit and life (John 6:63). They inform the soul and the mind. They give hope and direction. They change our outlook from one of submission to one of affirmation, insistence, and inquiry. They give the expectation of eternal life because God has chosen to create human life, which he is not going to abandon. He will do everything to restore it by removing the moral dilemma through Christ's sacrifice and physical death and through the resurrection. From God's running after Adam to sending prophets, from Jesus Christ, and finally from the Holy Spirit, we encounter a God who wants to repair all broken parts in a creation that is precious to him.

Human life informed and corrected by God's Word is the basis for greater human security and wealth where the Bible has been taught, understood, and applied. This informed view is not only true concerning what we know as the Western world. Wherever people anywhere have believed and applied the Bible, their lives have gradually changed. In the same geographical context, with the same resources, at the same time, people will be either poor or have enough by honest means. The deciding factor, most of the time, is what they understand about themselves on the basis of the Bible or from pagan texts. The Mennonites of Paraguay managed better than their native neighbors because of their biblical outlook on life.

The constant need of people is not only material in nature but also spiritual and intellectual in nature. Our bodies need physical food, shelter, and clothing. Our spirits also need nurturing. The Word of God addresses habits of life that affect our choices, and choices combine to form character. The Bible encourages work, imagination, and commitment and challenges us to excellence in art, work, and life. It demands honesty, industry, moral conduct, and exactness. Jesus Christ is not only involved in our justification and our good works in soup kitchens and homeless shelters but he also builds our character by calling us to moral and intellectual repentance and by calling us to fulfill our purpose as human beings in a real world of time and space.

The Word of God gives motivation, compassion, and skill. It encourages daring and enterprise because humans are made in the image of a good God and called to struggle for life against the normality of death. The Bible alone calls people out of an attitude of resignation, insignificance, and fate. Greater than what is normal in the natural universe is what the Creator calls people to seek and to do. The Bible addresses human beings as significant people, whose minds must be trained and whose consciences must be educated. Their ignorance is diminished, their understanding broadened, and through them the world becomes a different place than what nature, left to itself, would repeat in endless cycles.

There is a battle to be won against human and natural evil, and the armor and weapons come from God (Ephesians 6). Only in God and his Word will we find the necessary resources and compassion to recognize pain and sin *and* to struggle for a life of surplus in order to live and to help others in need. Scripture also provides us with real hope, wise counsel, and constant encouragement to serve God in his battle for redemption and restoration through Christ's work in us. Far from suggesting that we should seek a spirituality of resignation and acceptance, God's Spirit informs us how and where to resist evil in its many manifestations.

Failure to see that biblical ideas about all of life are the ultimate resource for the human being will lead to a faulty analysis of human poverty, for much of poverty is not the result of theft or catastrophe or natural conditions. Instead, there exists a poverty of ideas when human life is seen as an accident of nature or as a play of God. This worldview will inevitably lead to poverty in economic, intellectual, social, and physical dimensions. Even when natural resources abound, people can still fail to find them or to make use of them. The people will remain poor because of the destructive religious views they embrace. Any effective help from God and human beings must arrive in the form of material and spiritual resources together. The body and the mind must both be fed. Food for the stomach needs to be grown on what is food for thought first.

Where nature's spirits are believed to control human life, there can be no true spiritual life for people. Only from the outside vantage point of the God of the Bible, communicated by his Spirit to ours in the form of understandable language, can hunger and thirst even be acknowledged as problems within the otherwise normal workings of a fallen world. All other religions placate these experiences by teaching that a virtuous, spiritual attitude of submission should deny them as problems.

Bread, Fish, and a Better Focus

Feeding on the Word of God will inevitably change indigenous cultures. This may be a thing of great sorrow to the student of anthropology. But each culture is to a large extent the reflection of the values and views of the people in it. God's Word comes for the purpose of changing all cultural views and their expressions that lead to inhuman results and the demeaning of people. For the same reason, we must seek justice and compassion in our own culture and, thereby, change whatever does not reflect God's truth. By the same principle, other cultures will necessarily be changed where their moral failings create injustice, suffering, and death as a result of their religious, social, and political patterns.

We must be glad that Christianity has transformed the pagan European cultures of Roman and post-Roman times into somewhat more caring, informed, and humane societies. There are few Goths, Merovingians, and Vandals left. We should not, however, become satisfied and stop the continuous transformation during our own moment in history. Instead, we must also seek the same transformation for any human society around us where God's Word has not been heard or where it has been given no power to turn people from their inhuman, faulty, and tragic practices.

If our help is only a more equitable distribution of material things, we betray the source of our wealth. We are rich because God has informed us of his purposes and of our identity and hope. He has helped us believe his words about himself, about us, about the fall, and about redemption. Without that information for our minds and souls, all material reality would be our prison.

Jesus called the five thousand out of the fatalistic context found in Nazareth. He was not just one of them. The Son of God was in their midst, not just the son of Joseph. He called others to see that John's teaching at the court of Herod was not folly that led only to a beheading. There is a real righteousness, a basis to oppose evil. We do not live in an absurd world without a future judgment. To both groups, Jesus made clear that the solution was not an alternative political realm. He rejected their attempts to make him king by force at this time. There was no room for a utopian vision, a social program to meet all human needs in a fallen world. They came back for more, but Jesus refused and called on them to believe in him.

That "more," beyond apathy or excess, is to know Christ and to apply his Word that informs each person about all areas of life. His Word breaks the resignation response to the harshness of life in a fallen world. It informs us about the moral stand against hideous immorality in the lust for power. But it also tells us that there is no room for a kingdom of God on earth by human effort. Christians are called to prevent what is evil, not to impose what is perfect.

People who have been informed by the Bible have been able, in due time, to put enough food on the table, to substantially heal broken bodies and relationships, and to struggle for better governments. It has never been perfect. It will not be, until the King of Kings returns. All efforts to impose a perfect human kingdom, as Hitler, Lenin, Mao, and Pol Pot, as well as many Third World dictators tried to do, have been dramatic and horrible failures at tremendous human cost. Believing God and what he says about Jesus Christ also involves believing that we wait for the kingdom from heaven rather than installing it with our sinful visions. There is no room for utopias in the Christian world. But there is a righteous future ahead and a call for righteous acts and attitudes in the present.

3

A Community of Character

As the sun rose to another day, a cluster of men and women pressed tightly around the warehouse fence. This was the day they had waited for. Help had been promised. Backbreaking work in little plots had previously led to only scanty harvests. The effort withered when the rains refused to come. The land dried out; the cracks in the soil did not come from new shoots breaking through to the light of the sun, but from too much sun drying up the fields. There was little hope that this season would bring a fuller harvest.

But now water was going to be brought to the village from the hills, where it was collected through the rainy season. Rather than waiting for the rains, which often failed to come, the villagers were going to be able to tap a new source of stored water. Water, that softener of soils and solvent in every plant's search of nutrients, was going to flow to each plot of land and field.

When the gate was opened, tools for digging were distributed. Weighing them first with their fingers in the balance between hoe and handle, shovel and shaft, the adult villagers quickly turned their hesitation into admiration and went to take their places in a long line with others. Starting at the top, they began to scrape, hit, and dig a trench in the rocky ground. From the little dam in the creek that created a reservoir above the village, a channel was opened in the direction of the fields around each house.

Advice and skill from more experienced people with a different view of life, nature, and responsibility had brought a carefully designed program to replace more traditional patterns. They had heard of the dramatic need for a steady supply of water where nature provided the liquid from time to time in favorable seasons but often withheld it when it was sorely needed. From the perspective of an incomplete and even damaged natural system of provisions, they saw in their minds that a connection to the resource could be made available through effort and creativity. The need, recognized as a problem to be solved, would now be met.

The guests had so far organized the storage, the flow, the tools, and the timing. They had also explained to each villager during the past few weeks in great detail how to connect the water with each place where it was needed. After initial doubt and even mistrust, the villagers had responded to the dedication of the guests, first with doubt, then with amusement, and then with trust growing into commitment. It had always been difficult for a foreign project to be embraced, supported, and then owned by a village where life is seen as the repetition of patterns, rather than a discovery or invention of new ways to be initiated.

It had taken quite some time to have the villagers understand the program and not to see it as interference, criticism, or possibly even magic. Compassion has to be matched to instruction about new ways and ideas so that insight can be gained. That knowledge should lead to acceptance of both the helping hand and the thoughts, ideas, and values that are extended in the human family from "foreign cousins" who live in another place with a different, more effective and coherent worldview.

This morning all had come to do their part, according to the agreement. People gathered as if it were for a fair, a birth, or the monthly visit of the medical doctor from the capital to bring comfort and relief from pain and sorrow.

You can reach the villages on the Alto Plano (High Plain) in northern Bolivia when you follow the road to the high rim around the bowl in which La Paz lies and then turn to the north, toward Lake Titicaca. Rather than forking off to the west and Peru, a road will take you, after a few miles, along the eastern side of the lake, past meadows where llamas pasture and reed boats carry fishermen out on the water to their daily work. Small huts by the roadside made of boards, metal, and plastic sheeting interrupt the journey. Here woolens are offered together with refreshments cooked over an open fire in half of an old oil barrel. After you cross a ridge, you see solid adobe houses clustered around the market, a small church, and a flagpole in a township. Beyond that you finally enter a high valley on the left between rolling hills. Few trees still stand around the homesteads. In the background to the east you see the imposing mountains of the Bolivian Andes, perpetually covered by snow. They rise still much higher than the thirteen thousand feet of the valley you have just entered.

We left the ruins of the old hacienda on our left. Until the late fifties of the twentieth century, the farmers in the valley were all in the service of the landlord who lived there. He gave fields and work to the natives. He also took the harvest to market, where farmers and their wives would try to sell the produce. If he had been a good man, he would also be concerned about the health of the peasants and the schooling of their children. In return for the labor of the men and women, he gave them a minimal existence and a community of care. It was not a model system, but it provided for each family both sustenance and law in a community.

A Community of Character

The division of labor was neither elegant nor necessarily just, but together they produced so much that Bolivia was a food-exporting country in those years. Together the lush lowlands of the jungle regions and the highlands of the Alto Plano fed the people and produced more to sell abroad.

The land reform in the sixties abolished the hacienda holdings and distributed the land to those who had worked the fields, often for generations. The quasi-feudal system was replaced. But gradually the division into individual family holdings showed how little a family left to itself knew about the many diverse aspects of farming. Planning, crop rotation, seeding, fertilizing, growing, harvesting, and marketing could not all be overseen by each family. The land became poorer; the victory of land reform programs produced a catastrophe of envy, fear, and increasing poverty. The earlier greed of the landlord was passed on and multiplied to resurface as the greed of each individual family and fear toward their neighbors. Trees, always rare at this altitude, were cut for firewood and fencing, since each family needed to protect its holdings from the incursion of neighbors.

Today the men and women lined up to dig the first irrigation ditch. More water was needed in a regular flow to increase the crop production. This program had been organized by a relief and development agency, which, like so many, wanted to engage the villagers in the effort rather than doing the work for them. Villagers would learn the reasons, the mechanics, and the necessary effort required and then be able to copy it in other places. They would own the system that would immediately bring economic benefits through richer harvests and speak about a different view of the human being in harsh surroundings. Resignation to nature would be replaced by the initiative that results from people seeing themselves as more than a means of production or simply figures in the landscape.

Self-help programs like this one instruct people in projects that will increase their food production. Rather than laborers having to invest work and time in only the hope of a future reward, such programs pay workers up front in the form of food for the effort invested toward greater harvests in the seasons ahead. This is the normal pattern in the so-called food-for-work programs widely advocated and often beneficial. The idea is to encourage people to see what they can accomplish to meet their own needs. In addition, they own the project they work on and are, therefore, more likely to maintain it. It shows them directly the significance of their efforts. The improvement of their lives by their own efforts demonstrates to them how much they can accomplish and how valuable they are to each other as a community. There is an almost immediate return for the effort, and they see the results of their extra efforts in greater benefits within a short time.

Whereas normal subsistence farming gives individuals no ability to increase their yield, to irrigate fields, or to calculate which crops would sell for a higher price, these programs set people free from the daily need to procure food just to survive. The food is provided from outside in return for work so that farmers are able to invest work into a greater future result. Commodities of time and labor are transferred into food and cash through which doors are opened for a healthier and more secure and varied life. After a little time, life would consist of more than survival.

This morning the program is once again carefully explained to each participant. The work for future irrigation is given in return for the immediate benefit of food for each farmer today. Once the water begins to flow and irrigate the fields, there will be increased harvests. The food today is payment for the work done today—no work done, no food provided.

There are numerous situations in which this careful scheme is not understood. It is instead seen as a peculiar way for relief agencies to distribute food. You often hear remarks similar to these: "They insist that we work before we eat. All right, we will. We don't quite understand why the food is not handed out right away. But if they insist . . ." Frequently the work stops as soon as the food for the day has been distributed. The explanation will have to be repeated once again.

The ideas behind efforts are often not clearly communicated or not fully understood. Many cultures live only within the practical realm of present success or failure, showing little awareness of the power of good and bad ideas. This represents a kind of materialism in practice, even when people live in fear or awe of spiritual forces—which are seen in light of their power and not their personality, their interference with force in people's lives and not their character. Materialism surfaces when food alone motivates people to work, walk, or just wait. Without the food as a motivator, people soon lose interest in the project, even when only a little more effort would have made the water flow. But real effort requires a degree of abstraction, of ideas believed, of values pursued, of time spread out in one's mind and used creatively to bring about an improvement.

Projects like these create community, food, and work for a while, but they also need to be understood with head and heart. The deeper relationship between effort and reward, between present work and future benefit, between personal responsibility and commitment to implement a good idea remains in the dark. It is outside of the conceptual framework of people whose only reality is the present and who have never lived in the context of personal responsibility to bring about changes.

In the absence of a sense of responsibility for the good of others, it is virtually impossible to relate to a neighbor as a person in need. When destiny, fate, or gods are believed to be in control and everyone receives from them what they deserve, any change from the common patterns or even an intervention in the normality of life may be dangerous. Too much initiative will provoke the wrath of circumstances, nature, or neighbors who will object to such activism against traditions and the tribal consensus.

Likewise, the absence of a longer perspective than survival for today makes it extremely difficult to introduce the idea of sharing work and effort in a system of the division of labor for a future result. In cultures where the future is always a repetition of the past and never anything new, the promise of tomorrow as something new, different, and hopeful is outside the conceptual framework. It requires a shift from a cyclical view of history to a linear one, from resignation to entrepreneurship, and from fate to the God of the Bible.

In most cultures people live only in the immediate now. In their lives they tend to repeat what has been done before. Patterns are their security by helping the people conform to the known expectations and confirm partnerships in the collective memory and practice. We are familiar with that idea from Greek thought in which history was also seen as a cycle without purpose or advance. Greek tragedy is known for its ability to show how much human beings are caught in the effects of activities of gods and the Fates. People with cyclical worldviews may dream about a better world but know of no way to make it real. For them the real world already exists, and in it people are like leaves carried along on the river of passing time. Each has his or her allotment of events.

Then they are suddenly exposed to people from outside the tribe or tradition. They will usually listen with curiosity about ways other people have managed to be different. The wish for a better world brought in from the outside is native to our humanity. But the desire to do something to help themselves is, all too often, hidden behind the fear of trying something new under the critical and envious gaze of hidden spirits and next-door neighbors.

Where there is no present stability, no trust or confidence in the circle of greedy neighbors or in a distant government, life becomes a series of raw experiences. Government and fate, neighbors and nature have been cruel. What little love there is beyond natural affection and sexual attraction quickly melts away through attrition. When there is no god to trust, there will also be, with a harsh nature as your closest neighbor, little hope for significant changes in experience or in worldview.

Yet these precious peasants will reach out to any material help offered. Few of them, however, admit an equal need, beyond material things, in the realm of ideas and moral change. And few believe in their ability to help themselves through a change of convictions and attitudes.

A look into many of the welfare cases in our own context may reveal surprising similarities here. Welfare is now under review in many places in order to find an alternative. The old way created too many dependencies. Formerly the social services of the church and of the state were understood as assistance to deserving poor in times of emergency. But then a subtle shift in perception set in, which corresponds to a change in worldview. Help became perceived as an entitlement for the long term.

Christianity places the emphasis on personal need, both moral and material. We stand before God and in the middle of history, where judgment will take place. Individual life has significance, and all actions matter. We are called to create a life through work, education, love, and commitment to God and our neighbors. Yet when unfair conditions, natural disadvantages, and hardships arise, temporary help from others in society is gratefully accepted in order to find solid ground under one's feet again.

This biblical view affirms the existence of a good God and lousy conditions in a fallen world. It has always and in all places changed views of resignation and insignificance into an awareness of calling and responsibility. It has created an attitude of pride in personal work. Yet today this view has been largely replaced by a belief that the universe is impersonal and that all history is a flow of powerful events and circumstances. For the enterprising person, calling has been reduced to self-affirmation or private tastes without responsibility.

For others, calling has been replaced by an impersonal destiny, fate, and victim status. Responsibility is admitted only in the form of an obligation for others to provide equal access to material things in life for all.

This change in perspective reigned and controlled a whole generation with entitlement programs. It was then rarely discussed or understood. As a result, something uniquely human and stimulating has been lost. It is even worse when people whose worldview is supposedly rooted in the Bible encourage this generation of entitlements, of rights without obligations. Motivated often by genuine compassion for those in need, they propose a solution in the form of materialistic justice by focusing on quantitative concerns (an equal number to each), regardless of personal, intellectual, or practical effort.

They, in fact, undermine any significance of the individuals they seek to help. They want to provide food and shelter—noble intentions indeed—but rob people of the need to build a lasting shelter in the manner instructed from the Word of God. Their justice has little to do with the just rewards to different efforts in different moral and cultural settings. Their sense of justice accuses an unequal distribution and assumes that all differences are immoral. Equivalence in personal value is extended to demand equivalence in the value of any work, regardless of effort, skill, danger, responsibility, or cost.

Yet the idea of mathematical equality destroys the reality of personal, moral, and cultural inequalities. Its great concern is with a numerical outcome as the end result, but it neglects the fair results of unequal contributions, viewpoints, and practices.

The benefits of a Christian worldview—which encourages us to work with our hands to have enough to share with others (Ephesians 4:28)—are considered unfair because we will always see different results to different efforts, situations, and chosen priorities. The pursuit of material or mathematical equality assumes that all religions are only private concerns without public consequences. But what a person believes and then chooses always leads to different personal and individual consequences, which will be "unequal." The emphasis on and the pursuit of material justice dilutes the recognition of often painful, but necessary, moral distinctions in human experiences as a result of moral justice. The quality of the fruit speaks loudly about the roots, soil, and health of the tree.

After all, wealth and poverty can be the result of a faulty or ineffective legal system in which thieves steal with impunity. They can also be the results of different natural conditions and available resources. And they can, furthermore, be the results of unfounded, irrational, and inhuman religious and cultural practices.

The early church, whose life and expansion is described in the book of Acts, grew out of apostolic experiences and teaching and the powerful presence of the Holy Spirit after the day of Pentecost. Luke, who as Paul's amanuensis wrote Acts, continued from where he left us at the end of the third Gospel. During his many appearances after his resurrection and until his ascension forty days later, Jesus reminded the disciples of the Father's promises. They would receive power from the Holy Spirit to be his witnesses in Jerusalem, in Judea and Samaria, and in the entire world. The ascension of Jesus was not the end of God's presence on earth. The Spirit would come and be the dynamite by which all believers would overcome the strong opposition that would arise.

By many signs and wonders this promise was fulfilled throughout the length of Acts, which ends shortly before Paul's death. This history of Christ's work in the early church gives us sermons, discussions, tense moments, and fearful events with wonderful—though not always physical—deliverance of the believers. The truth of the gospel is not merely spiritually effective in the hearts and minds of people. There is also an external, historical reality as well to all of Christianity.

The book of Acts is a rich well from which we can draw illustrations in the life of the church and drink encouragement for our moment. The way God blessed his church in those years makes us long for the same in our times. We often crave those same signs and miracles to relieve us in our difficult situations. We are swept up with what went on then. We long to be the continuation of what happened following the Lord's death and resurrection.

At the time of the Reformation in the sixteenth century, many looked to the life of the early church as a model for the church at all times. The confusion, the immorality, the political instability, and the divisions within Christendom encouraged the longing for what, from a distance, must have looked like an easier, more harmonious time of church history. Back then, God added to their number daily; and they formed a community of those who had all things in common, sat under the teaching of God's Word, broke bread, and prayed together.

In fact, many in the Anabaptist movements of the sixteenth century believed that there had not been any true church since the apostles' work centuries before. They set out to re-create the early church according to their own vision in Münster, in parts of Switzerland, and later in Pennsylvania and in Canada.

Today many look again to Acts as a model for the church. They interpret the summary descriptions about the church in Jerusalem as admonitions for our current practice. Historical realities in the early church are turned into models for current social and economic programs for all human beings. In some Christian communities, singular experiences found detailed in the book of Acts are used to justify curious, universal doctrines. While history can serve as example, it can never establish good and proper action.

It is easy to forget that the church described in Acts had problems with both doctrine (what was taught and believed) and morality (how people lived). These were serious concerns and received much apostolic attention and correction. They were a central reason for the writing of the New Testament epistles, in which mistaken views were elaborated in detail and confronted with the corrective of apostolic teaching.

The present frustration inside and outside the church with less-than-perfect situations, with divisions and some confusion, and with unsolved social tensions and economic problems in the wider life of the community leads many to look to earlier models and pictures of a better world in the book of Acts. Quotations from the Bible are used to examine present conditions. Texts are cited to substantiate a mandate, to judge society's failures, and to promote justice through social programs modeled on what we have as summaries of early church life.

To what extent is this justified? Which elements of the New Testament church should be models for the present? How is the church described there? The discussion of social responsibilities toward the poor is often rooted in passages from the Old Testament (the Exodus, the Year of Jubilee, and the Year of the Lord's Favor in Isaiah 61) and from Acts in the New Testament. But is this understanding justified?

The dramatic and powerful work of the Holy Spirit in Jerusalem (Acts 2) brought many to see the real person and work of Jesus Christ. In Jerusalem Peter contrasted his earlier betrayal of Jesus with a powerful sermon about the crucifixion and resurrection. These events had occurred in the city only seven weeks before, and the evidence was still under their noses, or rather gone from under their noses. The tomb was

A Community of Character

empty, the eyewitnesses still in town. If factually in error, the claims could have been refuted. The chapter concludes with a description of the fellowship of the new believers: "They devoted themselves to the apostles' teaching and to the fellowship, to the breaking of bread and to prayer. . . . All the believers were together and had everything in common. Selling their possessions and goods, they gave to anyone as he had need. Every day they continued to meet together in the temple courts. They broke bread in their homes and ate together with glad and sincere hearts" (Acts 2:42–46).

In the fourth chapter we read a further summary: "All the believers were one in heart and mind. No one claimed that any of his possessions was his own, but they shared everything they had. . . . There were no needy persons among them. For from time to time those who owned lands or houses sold them, brought the money from the sales and put it at the apostles' feet, and it was distributed to anyone as he had need" (Acts 4:32–35).

These are descriptions of a richly changed life. Here is a real community of believers who are united by what they believe, what they seek, and by a concern to meet the need of some by the generosity of others. It seems a wonderful and spiritual solution to a recurring problem with wealth and poverty in the human family. The description of the real church in Jerusalem is, therefore, used to advocate the principle of sharing to arrive at equality. If everyone acted in this same way, we would eradicate poverty. Out of a sense of love and for the sake of justice, people share their possessions with those in need. They can then all have enough, each according to their need.

No wonder that it has sometimes been suggested that Marx advocated a Christian view of society with his proposal "by each according to his ability, for each according to his need." There are, however, in the context of the passages themselves, certain limitations to the harmonious image the description creates in our minds. We easily get caught up in wishful thinking from a desire to resolve painful inequalities, rather than apply biblical teaching faithfully and coherently.

The early church was a body of believers who submitted to the authority of Christ and his Word. Together they submitted to one discipline to be instructed, encouraged, and corrected. They devoted themselves to the apostles' teaching (Acts 2:42). This teaching was expanded as the need arose, and some of it can be found in the epistles that follow the book of Acts. Followers became disciples in their belief and in their practice. This community was a result of what they believed and their awakening to personal responsibility. This community heard additional teachings from Paul and others about salvation by grace and the moral responsibilities of each person to practice the Christian life. They heard about marriage and purity, about work and idleness, and about life and death.

The result was a community of believers whose lives were changed but not perfect. Acts *describes* for us their reality, but it does not *prescribe* a system of distribution. The passages describe that believers distributed their goods in specific situations of human need. However, historical developments do not imply doctrinal obligations. The sharing of wealth was not to become the normal way of providing for the poor. While these believers sold possessions and goods to support others, they continued to meet in their homes, which they did not sell (Acts 2:46). The picture is one of generosity and love, not of a new systematic stand against private property.

The same is found in the fourth chapter in connection with what follows in the fifth. "No one claimed that any of his possessions was his own, but they shared everything they had" (Acts 4:32). Personal property still existed, although they freely shared it. There was no hawking of possessions. Rather, it was something like an invitation "to make yourself at home while you are in my home." When money was needed, things were sold and gifts were made to the life of the church.

A married couple named Ananias and Sapphira lived in this community (Acts 5:1–11). They decided to sell their property for the benefit of others in need but then pretended that they received less than they actually did. They were under no constraint to give away everything (v. 4). They were not taken to task for giving only a part of what they realized from the sale of their piece of property. Their sin was deception.

They lied about the amount they had received for their sale. They were free to benefit from the sale of the whole and to give only a portion, whatever they wanted to give. But they were not free to lie about it by pretending that their donation was all they had realized from the sale.

The character of people—not mathematical or equal justice and automatic or compulsory sharing—is the point of these passages. Christians in the early church, as well as later throughout subsequent history, loved in practical terms. Old barriers of status, importance in the community from money or heritage, receded in the measure in which the gospel changed people to care for their neighbors' needs. These needs were material and spiritual. They included intellectual needs and training for a life that pleased God and benefited society. The occasions of being together were used for the specifics of teaching, learning, Communion as a celebration of Christ's death, and prayer.

The believers in the early church were in training to become disciples. Old habits were reviewed and transformed in light of the insights gained from God's Word and work in history. For this reason it is not strange to find between the two passages mentioned above in Acts 2 and 4 the account of a needy man, a crippled beggar, who was not simply invited to join a Jerusalem soup kitchen in a disciple's house. This man was told that he could not expect to get silver or gold from the disciples (Acts 3:6). Peter offered to give him what he really needed: "What I have I give you. In the name of Jesus Christ of Nazareth, walk." Peter helped him up. The man's feet and ankles became strong, and he leaped around and praised God. His real need was to know the existence and power of the God who healed him and then to faithfully live a normal life.

He is much like the beggar in Luke 18:35ff who addressed Jesus as Son of David and requested that he might see. He did not ask for another handout. He had had those for years. He wanted to see. Seeing would enable him to stop begging. It would change his dependence on the handouts of others. He wanted to see the Promised One, and that in turn would give him a different outlook on all of life.

Peter did not carry the crippled beggar to the early church where he could get free food from generous disciples. Peter's initial concern was not to give this man the experience of other Christians and their changed lives. The man did not primarily need community. He was not a victim of people's greed who needed to be introduced to his rights and benefits as a victim.

Instead, Peter brought him to Christ so that he would be healed in both body and soul. The focus was on the One who could heal rather than on what the community could do for him in physical ministry. Both body and mind needed attention. His problems needed to be dealt with and that included his intellectual problem. The way he thought about life and significance needed to be corrected by understanding that Jesus is not an idea, but the Savior, the Son of God. This God calls us away from resignation and poverty and invites us to make an effort to work. We enter into a covenant partnership to pray and work for the coming kingdom in which human beings will be permanently delivered from sin and death.

The beggar who asked for a lesser gift was given the greatest gift. His thoughts about life were changed; being given a larger coherent context in which to understand his place and purpose as a human being awakened his dignity and responsibilities. He became a disciple and found a new ethic for all of life. The heart of the disciples' teaching did not focus on their new personal lives, their changed patterns, or their new community. Instead, their focus remained Jesus Christ, who is Lord of all of life. The account in Acts 3 stands out between the two passages about the Jerusalem community. With all the wonder of what was happening in the new community, this man was being told about something more important—his basic intellectual and moral need of Jesus Christ, the Son of God.

There is more to reflect on in this immediate context in Acts, since the beauty seen in the passages of chapters 2 and 4 is quickly blemished. In Acts 6, serious problems crop up. As the disciples grew in number, some in the crowd were overlooked in the distribution of food. Consequently, the Jerusalem church chose deacons to address that problem. The

A Community of Character

nice picture of a sharing church is spoiled by problems of neglect, resentment, and partiality.

This should come as no real surprise to us. While the preaching of Christ leads to salvation and a changed ethic, the human situation created by that ethic is never perfect. Broken human beings and a damaged creation will mark all of life until "kingdom come." These Scriptures, and many others, show us that the early church cannot serve as a model of perfection. The perfect truth of Christ is our hope. Such hope is not found in the struggle to live the Christian life but is the reason to struggle more eagerly. The life of the church is not salvation. The church should not be set up as the model solution for human problems. There is no human utopia available to us.

We easily fall for the temptation of pursuing our vision in terms of what we think the gospel should accomplish. We crave a perfect world in which all people benefit. However, the warning of the Bible is that this is not achievable. There will be no visible kingdom until the King comes. Christ will change us then and produce a perfect environment through his reign. We will not accomplish this with our current broken abilities.

A further note is important. Even within the early church of Acts, only those who believed in Christ shared all things in common. The community did not include unbelieving Gentiles or unbelieving Jews. The early church is not a model for a society in which each citizen lives according to his or her distinct and chosen priorities with quite distinctly different moral and material consequences. The effects of such "religious" distinctions are not simply wiped out by an equalizing social program.

Even the church with its common vision and worldview continued to be under the corrective ministry of the Word. How can their experience, fallen and imperfect as it was, be set up as a model for us? Acts describes what happened; it does not prescribe what should happen. Instruction continued to be given on moral issues, on personal responsibilities, on doctrine, and on needed insight. People can only have things in common if their ideas, their struggles to understand and apply the Scriptures, and their personal discipline in the central issues of life gradually become common as well. Where this is not the reality, any equalizing social or political program will merely perpetuate the erroneous and inhuman consequences of arbitrary worldviews.

We are bound to experience disappointments and raise false hopes if our invitation to those in need is not preceded by an invitation to join us in what we understand and believe. Remembering our own brokenness, we need to lead others to the Christ, whose Word informs and transforms. Where people receive the impression that they can join the church without joining the fellowship of character with the constant struggle to do justice, they only add confusion to sorrow.

Social programs built on the notion of equally shared wealth or poverty, on redistribution, or on the desire of corrective justice by redistribution rob recipients of the need to examine their views and practices of life.

Traditions, habits, and rituals are never just luxuries or distractions. They all need to be examined in light of the reality they produce. Where they fail us we need to ask further about the Lord of reality and then bow to his Christ. Under the discipline of this Lord, the Creator of the universe, we learn about the shape of reality and the meaning of life. Humanity, meaning, and morals have their origin in God's choice to create us in his image and to address us in our minds. Fellowship with him must be found before we can join the imperfect reality of human fellowship.

Finally, I have often wondered whether the poverty of the Jerusalem church in later years—when Paul collected alms in the other churches for the poor in Jerusalem—had anything to do with the readiness with which the early church sold all things and gave to the poor. They possibly delighted in the experience of their new community so much that they became unwise, unscriptural, and finally unable. Being pleased with what they had at present while they could afford it, they lost sight of the other lessons to be learned in discipleship: responsibility, humility, and working by the sweat of the brow in a fallen world.

When you give away capital rather than interest and

benefit, you cut the branch on which you are sitting. You may communicate to those very young in the discipleship of Christ that generosity in giving is the lesson to be learned. But are there not also lessons to be learned in responsibility, in the wise use of talents, in reflecting on how to gain a surplus in order to be able to give to orphans and widows and on what do to when seven lean years follow seven fat ones?

Good intentions and acts of mercy are necessary. But it is equally merciful, and in the long run more scriptural, to invest in character development, in changing attitudes, and in the responsible creation of wealth. Just as the wealthy are admonished to be generous, the poor are admonished to be materially responsible as they gain greater freedom from pagan and nonbiblical views. The Bible calls us all to a creation of life in all its parts, not just to a shared consumption of it until we die.

The food given as payment to enable farmers to dig the irrigation canal on the Alto Plano was an investment for future returns. It was also a lesson in changed perspectives, personal responsibility, and assertiveness. The human being is made in the image of the God of the Bible. He or she deserves more than being a victim of human and natural circumstances.

4
_____

Servants' Hearts and Skills

Asian hospitality is proverbial. The welcome in a hotel rivals what we imagine a welcome to have been in a home long ago. The coolness of the floor, the bags being whisked away, the drink offered, and the quiet presence of a servant to assist you in any expressed desire merge with the fragrance of exotic flowers and the serene demeanor of your host.

In many places in Asia you meet people who seem to know what it is to make a person feel comfortable. Their service is attentive, quiet, and without an expected reward. Service is kindness given in humility, offering the traveler repose from the heat, the dust, and the noise of the world outside. Errand boys fly to take a message. There is nothing you can do as a guest that would provoke the kind of corrective remarks, critical looks, or behind-your-back cackle you may receive in other cultures.

All effort is directed to make the stranger feel comfortable and to avoid all upsets. We delight in this and are surprised and satisfied. We like this attitude of service, a willingness to comply with our wishes and to serve us without regard to rights or to the time of day. We compare the new experience with our own culture of rushing around, driven by time constraints and always in pursuit of personal advantage. Though we may not like the image, we are interested in our own survival, arrogantly pushing for space, title, and advancement. We show little desire to be a part of a larger whole.

The peaceful and serene images and impressions attract us to consider, momentarily at least, another way of doing things.

However, stone must sharpen iron, and arguments are honed by debate. Competence is increased by competition, and whether a problem is solved is decided on the basis of results in the real world. Human sweetness and good intentions alone do not suffice to create and protect life, food, and safety in the dangerous and unkind world we inhabit after the fall.

Some forms of politeness are often a mere appearance of attention. In such a case you will never know for sure, because the host's real feelings and reactions remain hidden, for the most part. Perhaps you will discover them by accident when the master servant scolds the younger one or when a parent corrects a child. You may never find out whether a host has really remained silent behind your back. Generally, it is hard to get to know someone whose sole purpose is to please you and who does this by building up an image, an appearance of things.

We worked with local staff in an East Asian country and found them to be a group of hard-working people. Our hours were long, and the needed details for effective oversight required long searches, frequent visits to local offices, a willingness to work with bureaucracies, and the wisdom to refuse payments of bribes or "attentions." Programs needed to be checked, evaluated, and supervised. On a tight budget, decisions were often difficult, and favored commitments needed to be compared and possibly curtailed for a while.

It is always extremely difficult to deal with tough situations when Asian politeness enters a situation and alters it to such a degree that the real ideas a person may have remained hidden. In this culture the director's ideas must never, under any circumstances, be insulted, hurt, or exposed as unimportant. A genuine discussion of thoughtful people is hard to achieve. The trained mentality is toward making peace and not disturbing the waters. People must not upset others.

This becomes complicated when you depend on the advice and counsel of local people. You employ them for their knowledge of the language, the land, and the people. You depend on them, yet the customs of politeness prevent them from speaking their mind when that seems to contradict yours. The directness and precision of Western speech are considered rude. All harsh angles of reality are rounded off, and great sensitivity is required to understand the hidden meaning of words or silences or facial expressions and body movements.

Real problems may arise when you wonder whether a job has been completed. There are always affirmative, admiring remarks, but you may never know for sure whether they are true to fact or true to feeling. "Was the letter sent yesterday?" "Yes" will always be the answer, not because of deceit but because your peace of mind and comfort are of first and greater importance than what happened to the recipient of the letter far away. The recipient can wait, but your peace of mind, here and now, is more important.

Foreigners especially are told what is thought they may want to hear—pleasant things, undoubtedly, but not necessarily truthful things. This is not because truth does not matter. Instead, truth as a concept does not relate much to the world around us. According to Buddhist teaching, reality is finally an illusion, and, therefore, truth does not describe a relationship between perception and reality. Truth is more like a manner of being, a detachment from pressure and concerns, a desirable personal state, and an experience of pregnant nothingness. It is not a defined reality out there in the world of facts to which I must submit. Appearance and impressions are more important; the experience of the moment needs to always be pleasant.

In some way I am reminded of this mentality when I see a Hollywood movie about what I assume is the life of Mozart, JFK, or the von Trapp family (as in *The Sound of Music*). To my surprise, disappointment, and some element of horror, I then discover that the facts are quite distorted for the sake of giving me a more pleasant or exciting movie experience.

Hollywood justifies the contortion of circumstances, the alternative arrangement of facts, by referencing artistic freedom. In Asia it is more the result of ideas about reality itself. When, as Asian religions teach in so many different ways, reality and the pain it causes to the observer can be avoided through spiritual exercises, the honesty to discover the facts and to face them analytically has no merit and is not a virtue. Virtue is rather any help given to detachment and denial of the unpleasant, that is, the ability to make you independent of external facts in the pursuit of your and others' happiness.

In the Christian worldview we do not detach people from the reality they need to face. Human value is independent of the situations they may have caused. Human identity and intrinsic worth are not judged by appearances or accomplishments. People do not gain personhood by esteem, by birth into a famous family, or by final accomplishments. They are persons, by definition, from the moment of conception. People are truly human quite independent of what they do. Failure in an area does not destroy the intrinsic value of the person. It merely points out areas where attention and improvement are needed. The reality of grace provides a new beginning and furthers growth. In Asian culture you dare not lose face, for there is no way you can get it back again. There is no sin and, therefore, no forgiveness. There is only shame, and that must be hidden. When the appearance has been sullied, there is no way to wipe it clean again. There is no certainty that anything is solid behind the appearances. It is better to create an illusion, a feeling of comfort, than to tell the truth.

But we still enjoy those who desire to serve us with all of their genuine gentleness. Of greater service would be a closer representation of truth, facts, and reality. A butler like Jeeves (in the books of P. G. Wodehouse) often saves the day for Bertie Wooster, a somewhat uncoordinated remnant of the English upper class. Bertie gets into impossible situations, from which Jeeves has to rescue him. The true servant is like this. He will tell Bertie what the situation is, even if it includes a humorous and not-so-subtle reprimand about the foolish ways of his aristocratic master.

Servants were always under someone's command. Anthony Hopkins in *The Remains of the Day* played an excellent example of this. He was loyal, devoted, capable, and sensible.

Servants' Hearts and Skills

His role was necessary, even though sometimes unappreciated. Being a servant was then considered to be an honor. Much responsibility lay on his shoulders. Some households would not have been held together were it not for servants like him. Sometimes that was because of the size of the estate. Sometimes it was because of a lack in the master's capabilities. A good number of masters in history and in literature come across as rather foolish, uncoordinated, and inept.

Few of us remember servants personally. We have grown into a world of self-made people, where even the service industry consists of independent providers. The tip for waiters in restaurants has become their contracted salary, a part of the cost of the meal. It does not indicate appreciation for particular service, kindness, and thoughtfulness.

We have moved on and only look back with some shame and embarrassment at an age when many families employed personal servants. At times we may mix it with a bit of romanticism about the good old days. In our liberated and democratic generation we get a glimpse of servants in books and films about the life of nobility and the wealthy in the past. Our social conscience has won over our romantic dreams (though it may fail us when we face chores we don't like to do ourselves). We also recoil from a sense of violated rights when we are expected to serve others but rarely attribute such sensibilities to those who serve us: our neighbors or those who come to serve us "from the islands." The biblical command to serve and to pay well those serving us exists precisely because it is not natural to us.

Our ideas about servants may be shaped by a persistent shame over slavery. Pictures of *Gone with the Wind* come to mind with insight from more recently released archives about the brutality of masters against slaves. We may always associate servants with a curtailed freedom, with insults, and under the whim—sometimes the whip—of masters. A sensitive conscience finds it hard to admit that some people will voluntarily submit to another person's demands. Yet we all do it when we accept a job definition. In our post-slavery world, service is related more to sales and marketing than to a voluntary and contractual form of the division of labor.

It is more common in our age to define personal rights and to reject servanthood outright as a fundamentally unjust relationship between master and an assumedly exploited employee. We see it as a contradiction to our notions of personal sovereignty. We are above taking orders and see independence as an accomplishment. Even our children live like premature adults in an adult world, because we interpret their independence as maturity.

Consequently we rarely nurture friendships for life anymore, in order to avoid being called to serve others. Instead, we take charge of our own life and only date and relate, taking our cues, our manners, and words to describe children and friends from the animal practice of bonding. We dominate and come and go without responsibility or any sense of building a life. That would tie us down for too long. Jobs, locations, and marriage partners are frequently changed to maintain our independence in changing life situations. We are taught little more than commitment to our own career goals and advancements.

Several cultural factors contribute to this. Our appreciation for the self-made person grew with increasing distances from towns and more personal time at our disposal. The Home Depot has replaced the professional craftsman. Each person has access to detailed instructions for repairs and, by force of circumstances, has become a handyman. Climbing the social and the educational ladders has been the result and the characteristic of an emphasis on individual capabilities, self-esteem, and a general advance in democratic, equal opportunity. But it produces character closer to a Darwinian view of competing animals than to what is required of love, mercy, and compassion for a human community. Whereas, impersonal nature has the fit survive and the weak go under, a human society under the influence of the Bible is characterized by protection, support, and encouragement of the weak.

Increasing fragmentation into individualism tends to leave us underdeveloped in social relations. We rightly value individuals by seeing that they make historical choices, are creative inventors, and question unjustified claims of authority. Individuals often show us a way hidden from collective foolishness, the crowd, and the titled. Yet we risk going overboard when individuals become individualists and begin to see themselves without any obligation to anyone or anything.

Even reason, facts, and reality can be pushed aside in pursuit of individualism. Such persons assume the role of God, believing that they can define anew the world around them. Profit, marriage, love, and community rarely have common definitions anymore.

Living under the benefits of a revolution, distant though it may be, we easily turn all of life into a passage through revolving doors. We construct an imaginary world: nothing remains fixed; everything must be subject to review and redefinition. Neither language nor race, neither sex nor religion, neither title nor wealth determines a person's place. Accomplishments alone, regardless of how they are achieved, define personal standing. The servant is out. We are all in charge of our own renewable worlds.

For these reasons it is difficult to talk about a mentality of service, of servanthood, in a culture of democratic, economic, and philosophical independence. Personal rights take precedence over obligations to other persons. True servanthood in our society is considered subservience. The boss, the survivor, the athlete, and the independent person in a career are cultural models much more than Mother Teresa, the stay-at-home parent, or the nurse. Social workers are underpaid; and teachers, though entrusted with the education of a whole new generation, receive little reward. We like their stories but want to reach for the top ourselves in high-paying, advancing careers.

One of our daughters attended a private school that encouraged volunteer service in the community. When she decided to become a social worker in a drug rehabilitation effort, the headmaster's first and only comment was that there is no money to be had in that line of work. The new heroes are crowned simply for their monetary success and influence. Many sectors of our society have a high admiration for sports and entertainment figures. These examples of brawn and show, of acting up and acting out, give weak substance to the requirements of developing character.

Many grieve over this development in a competitive society and lament a loss of humility. But this is often inconsistent, if not insincere. Proud assumptions about our greatness and merit come to us early. Children receive praise for little more than standing up in front of class or simply doing their homework. They may be wonderful children but are not yet masters of a subject when they have barely begun. Effort is not the same as accomplishment. Self-esteem may not lead to, and certainly does not equal, competence. Self-confidence is no sign of wisdom. More often it reveals self-deception, tragically supported by parents and teachers. Wisdom deals with the reality of the human condition, of the shape of the world and other countries, of the causes of poverty, and of human history and limitations. Learning is needed to acquire such knowledge, and this is made more difficult when children's personal opinions are valued higher than their knowledge and their Internet skills more than their curiosity and doubt.

Even when the problem is recognized, the remedy is not always fittingly chosen. The remedy for arrogance is not humility, but more careful insight. Humility is no virtue unless it is useful in developing skills to serve others and ourselves. Otherwise, the arrogance of the indifferent is replaced by the humility of the ignorant.

A sermon once suggested that we need more secretaries and fewer managers and CEOs. Christians should be willing to be servants to others, rather than thinking that they know the answers to many problems. Reference was made to people exploiting their power to control others. Where title or position spells authority, it is sometimes based on external factors like seniority, power, and social standing and not on skill or qualifications. But in addition, the preacher said, we should be servants even when we have qualifications. We should put these aside and humbly take on the work of lower positions. In such cases we should pool, not direct, the suggestions of all concerned. We should step back and let others come forward. We should not assume that we know anything, but be surprised by the knowledge of others. We could all benefit from a bit more humility.

We acknowledge many situations in which someone has surprised us with a perception or insight we did not expect and that exactly solved a problem. In business and at home we should create a climate for truth and wisdom to surface from all sources. Sometimes, it is out of the mouths of babes that wisdom comes.

However, we also know that we are not equally trained, experienced, or knowledgeable. We cannot take each other's places. Members of a team may complement but rarely substitute for each other. A rotation's purpose is to take turns among equals, and it is not primarily an exercise in humility. Humility builds character, shows our willingness to serve, but it should not stand in opposition to skill, leadership, and taking responsibility. It has no place in the service of a real need. The need alone should determine who takes the leadership.

The admonition to be humble is great at all times. But we don't want to give it a false priority when a life is threatened or careful plans need to be drawn up to avoid a catastrophe. In a business, including that of helping others, there is no value in seeing humility as a priority. The mission of the task at hand is not to teach humility, but to develop and distribute a product effectively. Motives, attitudes, and positions of people working together play a lesser role than being able to work well and to get the job done.

Apart from that, the sermon also revealed an unflattering characterization of the life and work of a secretary. She (or he) is hired for her contribution as a gifted person trained to do her job well. Her sense of community or of sharing an experience is far less important than knowing enough about the matter under consideration. Her insight (a servant without any qualifications to serve is unemployable), not her presence, is decisive for the contribution. Qualifications are foremost job specific and only then also a matter of fitting in. A qualified person should not hold back from a desire to wait with humility for work orders.

Is the Christian called to deny his or her qualifications or at least not to make use of them? Does servanthood require self-denial? Should human relations—how much others like you or how much you share their interests—be part of a job description? Should people be hired because they qualify or because they are humble?

Two passages in the Bible are frequently quoted to address the call for servanthood. Jesus' own example of the foot washing in John 13 is used to admonish us to do likewise. Parallel to this, the "gnosis" passage in Philippians 2 is cited. Jesus lowered himself, we are told, even to death as a service to us. Such a mind to esteem others higher than ourselves should also be in us.

These passages invite us to a healthy hesitation about any insistence on what we think are our qualifications. A little humility should always be in place, and an admission of ignorance is called for when it applies. More than our position

Servants' Hearts and Skills

is at stake. The needs of the other person require us to step back when we are of little use, no matter how willing we are to render a service.

We, especially if we take part in the American culture, must admit to a history of much personal daring mixed with stories of snake oil sellers and tall talk. Our past records people being asked to believe things in the hope that they might one day come true. Settlements were inaccurately described in pamphlets to potential pioneers in order to attract them in the first place. What some have achieved is taken as part of the American dream for all, as if a wish could be realized through frequent repetitions of the vision. The dream about a better future may provoke some to work on its realization. Such projections will set the goal, stimulate the effort, and justify the means. The dream will become reality for some because enough people will work at it, not simply because they believed it. But many will experience great disadvantages and will be left with just another unrealized dream. It is hard to distinguish between what is actually within the realm of possibilities and what is fantasy. Daniel Boorstin gives numerous illustrations of such tall talk, such arrogance, and such wishful thinking in the second of his three-volume study, *The Americans: The Colonial Experience* (Vintage Press, 1964).

The ability to realize an imagined dream also means that we readily walk where angels fear to tread. We have had courage to face all sorts of problems and to seek solutions. We should not deny our pride over our accomplishments when we see the better results in many people's lives. Have we not served them by our effort? We have left behind traditions that confined people in the past, in pursuit of a better, freer present. And in many areas the results speak loudly. Our failures should be forgiven. If at first you don't succeed, try, try again.

In America you have the saying "The squeaky wheel gets the oil." In Russia everyone is familiar with the proverb "The tallest blade gets the sickle." Americans tend to dare, assuming that there is a solution for any problem, eventually. Russians lie low and wait and hope that no one notices them. The former is not always arrogance but expresses confidence. The latter is not humility but illustrates resignation, fear, and fatalism.

Many pursuits, however, have also had their share of foolishness and failure. A disturbing self-righteousness and self-reliance coupled with disdain for those who did not follow in the same path are also part of our history. People always dream and often claim to hear voices or to have visions. Sometimes drugs and other means, even religion, to escape the limits of the real world induce these. Yet dreams and a different kind of vision, in the Christian worldview, are not part of an escape effort, but rather part of a creative effort to transcend the here and now.

There is something remarkable about a worldview that not only has visions but also uses them to imagine an alternative and then finds ways to make it real in time and space. The whole European tradition, including its former colonists in America, Canada, South Africa, and Australia, has a history reflecting a mandate to continue creation and to correct faults in it. It encourages the mentality of do-it-yourself skills. Consequently, we honor the person who can manage a situation as Adam managed to give names to animals and to create a life together with Eve.

Such confidence from God's calling was required to tame the wilderness, whether among Germanic tribes or in uncharted territory during colonial times. There was no help available from others. Individuals had to look out for themselves. The open land in America—where settlements preceded the rule of law and settlers defined the law for themselves—was hostile until someone subdued it from an understanding of the dominion mandate.

That history is a mixed bag of good intentions, personal discipline, and high hopes. There are also crushing failures when enthusiasm naively assumed human innocence and "utopias" were imposed. Our intellectual and cultural roots in Athens, Rome, and Jerusalem refreshed the mandate to rule, to bring order, to emancipate us from destiny, and to improve the human circumstances as best we could. Judaism and Christianity encourage the creation of a new world, whether in the Promised Land, or later in Europe, or eventually on "new" continents.

But old problems from the fall of Adam are always present. The American dream of a new people was diluted by cruelty to Mongol or indigenous Americans and African Americans. We always live in the tension between efforts to realize high dreams and crushing awakenings. The assumption of innocence in the search for solving the world's problems has been hampered by real evil among us. Utopian expectations, even when at times unfulfilled, intertwine with times of isolationism and global relativism.

Recognizing all this, we often hear the suggestions that we should become more Christlike by abandoning what we think we know and giving ourselves to the demands of the world community. Are they poor? Then give and share, we are told, for it belongs to all equally. Do people or societies have problems? Then we probably caused them and should repent. Have we been successful in feeding our people and reducing early death? Then we probably accomplished this by consuming the world's resources; so we should abandon our lifestyle that brought these solutions at the expense of greater pain to others. Have we tackled problems by means of rational thought, material science, and law? Then we should become more spiritual, humble, and submissive in the community of religious experiences around the world to reduce the environmental effects of our advance.

Servanthood to some is the call to void exceptionalism. Being different, even when that is helpful, is seen as discrimination, because it sets others apart. Our success is seen as a flaw, because not everyone else shares in it equally. There is just no way to come out right. We are guilty whatever we do. If we are skilled and make use of it, others will accuse us of arrogance and oppression. If we don't use it, we are heartless.

Paul with his physical disability was variably accused of lacking perfection. He was too authoritarian, too short, too untrained in rhetoric—too anything, so that what he had to say would not have to be listened to. In our day we would have asked Paul to be more of a facilitator and otherwise remain silent. He should be an apostle of acceptance, not instructing us on what to think and how to live. That would have satisfied the Corinthians who had accepted every imaginable and contradictory view in their midst. But their main problem was a lack of submission to expert, apostolic teaching; this, in turn, led to a lack of community, rationality, and discernment. The problems lie in their midst.

It will help us understand the problem people often have with biblical authority when we acknowledge that the Bible starts with a definition. God, creation, and purpose are set long before our arrival on the scene. We are free neither to invent a new reality in our image nor to humbly refuse the mandate to discern between truth and falsehood in any area. Objecting to a helpful solution is no virtue unless the solution prevents others from awakening to their individual potential.

I was once even accused of being unkind for showing a single person that I was engaged. It made others feel sad that they were not. A colleague once told me that he did not want to talk with me because I had answers to questions and had better arguments.

We easily feel guilty in such situations; they create tension. At times we should avoid them, for none of us is without fault. Such situations force us to examine our responses, our motives, and our attitudes. But we are in deep trouble when we park our skills merely for the sake of leaving people satisfied in their hole. They may feel happier, but they are no closer to the ladder that would offer them a way out of the pit.

I am not suggesting that we immediately reject the call for more humility and servanthood. We are called to an ethic of the extra mile. In the face of human pain and suffering, the wrong use of power, and the realities of greed and pride, we want to be sure to do what is right and honorable. We are called to be peacemakers, to turn the other cheek, to expect suffering for the kingdom, and to walk humbly with our Lord. None of us is there yet; so we try. We are slowed in our tracks when an accusation gets thrust at us. But we should not stop there unless we are objectively wrong.

Good servants are not those who resort to inactivity, to ignorance, and to being doormats. They are not the ones who get chased like rabbits from one end of the furrow to the other by the deceptive play of hedgehogs in a parallel furrow.

Instead, the servants in the Bible are wise and freely give from their wealth to those who depend on them.

The two passages cited before (John 13 and Philippians 2) show this with astonishing clarity. In both of them Jesus served others because of his unique ability, power, and calling. In fact, he does for us what no one else can do. His service is indispensable. Only he can accomplish what we need for our life and salvation. His generosity is tied to his unique person and to our unique dilemma. He is the Master and must function as such.

Peter initially refused to have his feet washed: "No, . . . you shall never wash my feet." Jesus' response revealed his exclusive skill and power: "Unless I wash you, you have no part with me" (John 13:8). It was essential that Jesus wash Peter, first in this foot washing and then in the reality of Christ's perfect service of the substitutionary death for the legal forgiveness of moral guilt. His compassion and service were expressed as a sign of his judicial authority. He alone could accomplish what was necessary.

Christ did not become humble here, abandoning in some fashion his position or power. This is no lesson in humility, but a necessary service for the lives of Peter and the other disciples. What they needed only he could provide. Without him they would have no part in the forgiveness of sin and in eternal life. There was no call for a committee, for sharing, or for a change of roles or assignments. The need was specific and so was the solution in the life and death of a chosen person, Jesus the Christ, Judge of the universe.

This should not surprise us. Often Jesus expressed the uniqueness of his abilities. His refusal to call on twelve legions of angels prior to his arrest by Roman soldiers did not express a submission to death. Jesus was not a pacifist who resigned himself to human wickedness and preferred death to life in the real world. He is not a symbol for those who willingly give up their earthly lives so that they might gain eternal life. He is also not the model for the martyr who gives up life to a cause, which will then be carried on by others. He is not the modern existentialist, showing us how death should be faced. He is not the hero who dies for his convictions.

All these attempts to interpret the death of Christ are not shared by him. He dreaded the hour and was troubled. But he knew the reason why he came to this hour (John 12:27). He came and went to that death because it was the only way to fight and win the war against sin and death for which he came to his own. He alone, the second person of the Trinity, could be the sufficient substitute for our sins. The Judge of the universe alone could take the judgment on himself. His death was a chosen stand in a battle for us.

He was uniquely equipped to fight and win. He served us as a master, prepared and deliberate. He did not humbly ask what we thought we needed or what we would like. He dared to tread where all else turned and ran. He became sin for us and nailed the curse of our sin to the cross in his own body.

Good servants are necessarily qualified for their jobs. They are in the privileged position of being depended on. The work of medical doctors illustrates this well. They serve their patients with skill, dedication, and courage. They dare to go where life is difficult. Their schedules are often inconvenient. They expose themselves to bacteria, to infections, and to the danger that the patients may die in their care. Their services demand a high level of training and skill.

Similarly, teachers do not primarily facilitate the self-development of children. Instead, they skillfully instruct and educate. Their task is to introduce and prepare students for the wider world with all its real shapes, discriminating requirements, and scales of accomplishments. Good teachers serve students by helping them to measure up to the demands of real life. They develop their students' competencies in the face of tough competition in exams and through exposure to the requirements of the job market in the real world. Teachers are like mentors who explain and love and go the extra mile in repeated exercise of patience in order to pass on to others the skills they have acquired.

It does not serve anyone to ignore the rigors of the real world. When the person who requests a service is ignorant or incapable, a humble servant is actually useless. Good servants should speak up and even contradict those they serve. If they do not, they merely reinforce the status quo of ignorance or incapacity. This is the effect of the Sesame Street view of theology, ethics, and aesthetics. Every challenge is turned into a game; and, by means of that game, the sharp distinctions are removed between family and friendship, between art and self-expression, and between culture and nature. This serves only the self to be a self. But there is a real world out there where the untrained self will not survive intact.

Jesus served us by applying his person to the task. In Philippians Paul showed how Jesus took on the form of a man while he continued to be God. Only because he was simultaneously God and man could he become the servant to go to the cross. The admonition to have the same mind in us is only obeyed when we see our skill as something to be offered in service to others. Then we can be a secretary or a manager (or anything in between) without seeing in jobs a higher or lower service potential. Each person is useful because of individual skills. Each is needed equally for different tasks. The mandate to regard others as higher than ourselves relates to our attitudes, not to our skills. It sets priorities of service over position and not of one skill over another. For that reason the Bible never suggests an inequality of the value in skills or callings but gives praise for a service lovingly rendered. God expects that each person's qualification be fully recognized, used, and valued.

Jesus served us from his superior position as the Son of God, never abandoning it in weakness and humility. Modern theology likes to speak of the weakness of God as something to be marveled at. They see in Christ's weakness further evidence that God is so different from human beings with their lust for power. But with this view, theologians do not express a biblical understanding of God and his work. Instead, they advocate a wholly other God, the *totaliter aliter* God of Emmanuel Kant and Karl Barth. The birth in the manger as a baby and the death as the innocent on the cross seem, at first sight, to justify such a focus on the weakness of God. But it seems to me to be more appropriate to see in such events the power of God, the determination to get a job done. Christ left his throne, not because of being demoted, but because of a job he desired to do for us that required a real humanity. He died in victory over a battle against sin and death. About his childhood we assume he loved and honored his parents. But in public we know nothing except that, as a twelve-year-old, he set straight the Pharisees and others in the temple.

When a manager serves an apprentice, it is not from a position of weakness. Instead, the experienced manager instructs the apprentice in the skills of the trade. A teacher serves a student by passing along learning skills and tools together with an explanation of why they are necessary for life in the real world. To teach spelling is not a sign of pride or power, but ultimately of compassion. The student should not see exam results as a sign of the teacher's authority, but of the teacher's valued ability to point out weaknesses in the student's knowledge. Learning to spell will enable an individual to read and write, to be understood, and not to be fooled by the small print in contracts.

The reason we need such a service by the one equipped to render it lies in the awareness that we live in a definite world already created. There are natural laws, which need to be discovered and respected. In the same way there are moral laws and societal conventions, which we need to acknowledge and respect for the sake of relationships and survival. There is a rational world out there, not a random world of our own imagination.

I am not denying that we all need the admonition to be humble and to render service. We are prone to take ourselves for the center of the universe. We have accomplished much already. The call to service is a needed reminder that without our help others will be poorly prepared to survive in the dimensions of the real world. Without the benefit of training, people are left to learn on their own through failure and pain. Should we sit back and let the real tragedy of life rule over those for whom we have had no compassion?

Servanthood is a choice to act from strength in the midst of much tragedy. Material needs, spiritual and intellectual confusion and error, as well as abusive power need to be confronted, countered, changed, and corrected. To serve our neighbor, to "wash one another's feet" (John 13:14), is a constructive involvement. It is at times subversive to false ideas and practices. It acts against the rule of death and raises a banner of truth, light, and love against the kingdom of darkness.

We are not called to politely accompany people through the tragedy of their lives, to hold their hands in their pain, but to enable them to change their physical and intellectual/spiritual environments in order to diminish that tragedy. Both cynicism about real evil (in other words, acknowledging it in all its pervasiveness) and passionate engagement to restrain it in our life and the lives of others are the core of real servanthood.

5

Worldviews in Collision

Colorful pictures and detailed descriptions of other countries bring into our lives glimpses of the daily experience of people in other cultures. Modern means of communication, news reports, and on-the-scene broadcasts expose us to both the wonder and the tragedy of human life. Little escapes our observation when the world is opened up and brought to our attention for admiration of diversity, for grief in times of catastrophes, for protest against evil governments, and for assistance in times of hunger, war, and natural disasters.

Human beings live in such real situations. They receive our attention because there are painful and immediate and visible results. We can relate to them when they are described, pictured, and brought into our lives through television and newspapers. We recognize with horror that people just like us suffer outside our immediate experiences. They are victims of war, natural catastrophes, and evil governments.

Much less visible is the fact that people are also affected by the way they see reality. Their manner of thinking about life and their loved ones, their attitudes toward nature, and their concepts of right and wrong may be very different from our own. And different views result in different actions and responses to a variety of situations. Some responses, born from a religion or worldview, may easily cause tragedy or worsen an already tragic situation. In such cases, that religion or worldview must then bear the brunt of the blame.

Reality does not only have a shape of its own; it is also shaped by our choices, by our intervention or neglect, and by our assumptions and actions. At home and abroad, people act on the basis of their ideas concerning all the recognized aspects of the real world.

Social work, as well as relief and development efforts, is not only concerned with objective hardships. Besides contributing labor, money, and machinery to strengthen the hands of suffering people, relief work must also address erroneous ideas about the real world that may have led to the catastrophe at hand. Intellectual relief must be brought to people who have no encouragement to think at all or who have false concepts that create suffering and other terrible consequences.

We recognize that a tree is known by its fruit. A similar relationship exists between what people believe and how they act in life's circumstances. It is not unkind to suggest that the fruit of faulty worldviews is found in the often poor and harmful way people deal with the world around them. When individuals act on the basis of their worldview, the results will show whether their view puts reality in focus or distorts it terribly. Worldviews are like the glasses I mentioned earlier through which people see reality. And when reality is not accurately viewed, the glasses should be changed.

The first step toward helping people out of their immediate need is material: food, shelter, and hygiene. And a second step must follow rather quickly. People require the development of their minds as well. It is a coping skill based on an accurate understanding of the world we inhabit. Material things have a form and a purpose. In the same way, all material needs have an intellectual/cultural component. To the old Chinese proverb "Do not give me a fish, but a fishing tackle" we would add an additional request: "Give me a reason why I as an individual person should live, by fishing or any other means."

The failure to encourage such reflection leaves the mind and heart malnourished and the personality underdeveloped. Yet unfortunately many cultures value reflection less than repetition and discovery less than tribal discipline. In most religions the individual person is understood to be the problem. The problem would be solved if people were to lose themselves, abandon critical thinking, and become one with all the rest.

Collective repetition is a characteristic practice in Marxism (as a secular religion) as much as in African tribal religions, Islam, or Buddhist chants. Religious teaching and traditional rituals focus on submission not only in the moral sense but also in the metaphysical sense. An individual is not sinful but a mistake, a misfit in the greater scheme of things. The problem is that people think too much, not that they do not discern enough.

Only Judaism and Christianity raise humans to the level of being in the image of God, rather than children or effects of natural circumstances. People are a little lower than the angels and have dominion over all creation, including nature, history, and a flawed life.

Human beings are the only beings who are not satisfied with merely living instinctually. We crave an explanation for life. We do not just accept things but wonder why. We try to analyze what should and should not be done. All other forms of life respond to the givens of the moment in a programmed form. But we seek an explanation and match or stretch what is to what ought to be. We think and act in the bounds of moral and philosophical categories.

In fact, while animals respond from instinct, we learn to question. We transcend the present moment—with its stimuli, dangers, and pleasures—to wonder how we got here, how we can live well, and what we must do to control the future. We raise questions about what is good, what is just, and what is beautiful. We gather information from facts and from ideas, including history (what people have done), philosophy (what people have thought), and geography (how people have lived).

Such categories are not just inherited. They are built from insight, past experiences, and different ideas. We may find better ideas in the experiences of others or through our own imagination. We will find justification or motivation from personal values or from external stimuli. Muslims live by the teaching of the Qur'an. Christians follow the Bible. African tribal religions follow the inherited stories and the dictates of the elders.

In each case, we find obedience to an accepted authority that governs decisions and describes life and what happens when one or the other choice is made. However, the Bible's emphasis has an additional factor not found in other religions. The exposure of the text of the Bible to the demands of a critical argument is unique. Or, to say it in another way, whatever the Bible teaches must be checked out against the requirements of logic, truth, and the reality of human lives.

Jews and Christians, in distinction to Muslims or African animists, do not bow in blind faith or obedience but argue for the sake of truth in light of what exists for all of people everywhere, what has been said before, whether promises are kept, and whether God is worthy to be believed and obeyed.

The additional factor in Jewish and Christian thought is whether reality supports the pronouncements of Scripture. The Jewish teaching about creation, the Greek influence in the pursuit of the good rather than just normal life, and the Christian faith with its central emphasis on the incarnation of God in Jesus Christ have made the traditional view in our background very different from what is taught in religions in general. We seek to know the created world out there so that we can thrive.

There is not just a story about Christ in people's minds that motivates them to live as he did. Instead, there has been the confidence that history is a purposeful continuum. God created a real world, and we are in the image of God in that reality. (Those of us who are married even live differently than Jesus did and thereby fulfill a creation mandate from God.) Christ came, died, and was raised in history. We live in that same space-time dimension, which has objective measures that are affected by our choices.

Our way of developing perspective in painting, our effort to measure precisely, to figure out which causes lead to what effects is directly related to the affirmation of an objective world in which we live and have our being. We are part of that objectivity, though we perceive it always as finite subjects in concert with others.

More recently there has been a shift in the concept of what is real. At times that shift has been very insidious. At other times it has been more deliberate and even selective, as when postmodernism is called on to justify personal opinions and to free them from the critique of others. The results soon become blatantly visible. They return us to the old communalist discussion of earlier days. It is a shift from reality to a vision of reality and from confidence to feeling good about the view held—whether it is true and fitting or not.

There is a parallel here to the loss of confidence that painters can give expression to an objective reality; they now paint their psychological states or their personal daring instead. Frequently they are more concerned with their own states of mind than their meditations on the state of the world, which they wished to bring to our attention in a more confident past.

When we distance ourselves from Christianity, we become more concerned about faith and obedience than about whether what we believe and do are true to the real world, the field of activity addressed by God's Word. We become more accountable to ourselves—whether we have been true to our innermost feelings—than to history, to the next generation, or to the living God.

Rather than adding to the story of the human race in the real world, with personal battles of how to lead a virtuous life in the midst of real temptation, each person begins to write his or her own story, individually defining what is good, beautiful, and profound. It has become fashionable and is accepted as a mark of humility to express a deep-seated hostility to all inheritance and obligation from the past. Solzhenitsyn speaks somewhere of "a stubborn tendency to grow not higher but to the side, not toward the highest achievements of craftsmanship and of the human spirit but toward their disintegration into a frantic and insidious 'novelty.'"

A similar slide to the side is found in the understanding of the core of Christianity. While faith used to be the acknowledgment of certain verities, beginning with the acknowledgment that God exists and rewards those who diligently seek him (Hebrews 11:6), faith has increasingly become mostly a personal matter. We make our own decisions about what to believe, or we fill old symbols with new, more personal meanings. The only requirement seems to be that we feel good about our testimonies concerning our good feelings.

But where God and creation have no specific forms or attributes, human life also has no direction or content. Rather than acknowledging the created form, people today tend to invent a religion that the past associated with paganism. Israel did this at the time described in the book of Judges and repeatedly later on, only to produce times of cultural chaos and depravity.

This shift from a wider, more objective view to a narrower, more personal view can also be described in this way: what was a concern for the whole human reality has gradually been reduced to satisfying material needs, leaving out any concern about the moral/cultural background created by worldviews and religions. The recent, more subjective emphasis sees religion as a private concern and of no weight in shaping the way people live with or under material conditions.

The shift has also affected what contribution Christians make in the context of Christian relief and development work in other cultures. Failure to recognize a shift here will lead, at first, to a denial of a specific and critical biblical ethic. Second, it will blind us to the tragic reality that occurs when a people's religion becomes for us nothing more than a cultural trait and inheritance. Without the critical evaluation of what that religion teaches and how it influences the values and choices of the people in need, the relief will distribute goods but not dispel faulty thinking. It overlooks the realization of a link between what people believe and the consequences in their lives. When worldviews are left unexamined morally and practically, their consequences in the choices of people will make the problems of life worse, not better.

People act on the basis of their worldviews. What we believe about people, about the use of time or the place and meaning of work, about life and death, and about nature and the eternal will express itself in our choices. Values are not mere components of a discussion or personal preferences in taste. They affect the way we think and the way we act. And the consequences soon follow.

The shift in thinking I mentioned above leads many to abandon any concern about whether people understand the created world accurately. The only remaining concern is how they feel about their beliefs ("I like it"; "That is how I do it"; "I personally believe it"). Personal opinions are presented as evening news. "How do you feel about it?" is the reporter's most common question concerning anything from the Olympic Games to the effects of war. If religion is believed to be a personal opinion, it will be regarded as a private matter. The love for multiculturalism as an idea will protect and preserve the right to a private worldview. Monty Python's *Life of Brian* could grant the wish to one man who wanted to "have the right to wish to be a woman." He would of course be forever unfulfilled in his wish. But so also will inhuman religions, social customs, and faulty worldviews fail to satisfy the human need for life, meaning, and security. We forget this to our peril. Religious views without any relationship to the real world of human beings, of history, and of life and death are not incidental luxuries for private contemplation. Often they are the cause of the human need in the first place.

The effort to help people materially must continue. They need the fish at first and then the fishing tackle to help them. Material needs are real and must be met. But if people *believe* in a worldview in which their needs are unfulfillable, unreal, or unavoidable, they will not believe that a change is possible. Where suffering is seen as normal, or as a part of the deeper and continuous experience of life, or even as the will of God, little resistance to suffering will be raised. Where nature is seen as the expression of the will of Allah or animated by spirits, nature's ways will always be repeated and never changed.

In addition to meeting material needs, the whole way of thinking about the real world needs to be changed in light of a more biblical view of reality. This is not merely a matter of having a few spiritual lessons attached to some material projects. Bible studies need to relate to the problems at hand. These studies should be a response to the religious and cultural views that lead to material disasters. Bowing before Christ involves a willingness to become his disciples in the ways we think, act, and live concerning work, relationships, authority, responsibility, and life—in opposition to any notion of fate.

Belief does create a vision, but visions can be dangerous when they neglect the perils of the real and fallen world. We should not live in a dream. Christianity includes the past, present, and future of the real world in one perspective. With this wider view we can be better informed for our choices. Belief can also be dangerous when it prevents us from seeking further knowledge. In our fragile lives we must at all times look at reality with open eyes. Our belief can and should be challenged by the real world and corrected by the "glasses" that bring together the words of God in the Bible and the works of God in creation, nature, and human beings.

Exposure to the real world should reveal a person's blind faith. Irrational faith is the reason for so much human misery in various religious contexts, including the religion of atheism in Marxist societies. A faulty faith cannot tolerate examination in the light of reality, for it is derived from a faulty vision rather than the relationship between the text and the context of real human beings.

Christians and Jews argue with the text from their experiences of reality. Using the text, they understand the world they live in and what they should do to improve it. In turn, the experiences of reality raise the questions to which only the open text gives a wide-angle view from the past into the future.

Christians live by more than bread when they obey God's Word after seeing that it does not invite blind faith. The Bible challenges us to examine the words of God in light of the real world: "Come now, let us reason together" (Isaiah 1:18). "Put your finger here; see my hands. . . . Stop doubting and believe" (John 20:27). More than five hundred believers testified to the resurrection (1 Corinthians 15:6). When the Bible is recognized to be the accurate description of the real world, it serves as the prescription for the choices and responsibilities before us. People with the Bible not only observe and respect what is natural but they can also choose to do what is moral to change what is natural in a fallen world into what is cultural or civilized. Their worldview, informed by revelation, contains a mandate to give a different shape to the world they previously saw only in light of nature.

The effect of biblical teaching has always been this call and profession of faith and action. In more recent times we have changed the center of the gospel from what God has said and done to finding a way to feel good about ourselves. We have replaced orthodoxy with "orthopathy": feeling right about what we wish to do.

Paul praised the Thessalonians for doing more than loving each other and feeling good about themselves, their situation, and their belief. Paul's work among them—for the few days before he was chased out of town—resulted in broad benefits. Proclaiming that "this Jesus . . . is the Christ" (Acts 17:3) showed up in their work produced by their belief, their labor prompted by their love, and their endurance inspired by their real hope in history. These are wonderful descriptions of a different way to live (1 Thessalonians 1:3). But evidently we have here much more than a remarkable lifestyle. A whole worldview had been expounded and had come to lie at the heart of their changed lives. When Paul wrote his first epistle to the Thessalonians, he could build on what he had taught them in person.

The historical record of 1 Thessalonians draws out for us many of the details of a Christian worldview. The church has not been left with a personal and private faith as a foundation for personal development. There is little room for opinions in matters of ethics. The full circle of life is seen in light of the Bible, rather than in light of either pagan culture or personal choice. Paul talked beef, not the trimmings of your choice. The meat was specific and more *mores* than morals. The effect was a different view of the world in all areas. A new pair of glasses was given with definite results in their perspective.

The relationships and characters of the Thessalonians changed when they believed Paul's explanations. Their faith produced work, their love prompted labor, and their hope in Christ inspired endurance. This was not the work of Paul. He had not brought them religion, but such a view of God and creation that they "turned to God from idols to serve the living and true God, and to wait for his Son from heaven, whom he raised from the dead—Jesus, who rescues us from the coming wrath" (1 Thessalonians 1:9–10).

I was not surprised to find in Russia the result of what was an idolatrous worldview with inhuman consequences in society. The magnificence of the churches within the Kremlin walls in Moscow cannot wipe out the use made of them by an atheistic regime for seventy years. While the artwork speaks of the resurrected Christ, the mummy of the regime's dead leader lies in state against the Kremlin wall a few feet away. Jesus' words were silenced, but Lenin's are still repeated daily.

Worldviews in Collision

Even the subway under the city streets, with its diverse and often very artistic stations, bears witness to forced labor and prisoners of war. The approach to the city's international airport takes you over the White Sea Canal, which took the lives of thousands of Russia's own enslaved people to construct it. And when you leave the capital with all its signs of power and grandiose pseudocathedrals in Stalin's triumphalist architecture, you follow the Russian road toward hundreds of provincial towns. Their hearts and histories have been torn out. Their populations live for the most part in uniformly gray, decaying apartment buildings made from prefabricated cement sections. All are heated uniformly from a central heating plant, and there are no valves on individual radiators.

The kindness and hospitality shown to me by my hosts were overwhelming. They sought to spoil me with the last of what they had for themselves. Yet I noted that their worldview was colored by a belief in a mixture of magic and materialism regarding change and hope for the future. Either the new market system or God and religion would bring the change. A strange marriage of science and mystery is the background of Russian popular contemporary thought.

Two systems exist in their perception of the scientific workings of nature, society, and the universe: Marxism and capitalism. Now that the first has been disavowed, the latter will replace it automatically, even scientifically! Using the same mentality, they believe that by replacing atheism with religion, God will mechanically improve their lives. In neither the physical domain nor the spiritual domain is there a notion of personal change, real choices, repentance, or gradual and persistent effort. The mentality is still materialist or mystical. Great discouragement set in when unscrupulous people easily took advantage of the moral, economic, and cultural vacuum. The expected has not arrived. Capitalism is still the game of the few, and religion "does not work either." But how can it, since the main players, the people themselves, have rarely understood the core of biblical thinking about God and humans or about history and our common responsibility in it?

Paul gave the church in Thessalonica a different view of the universe. God, who thinks, speaks, and acts, is eternal and alive in the place of many competing idols or an impersonal energy. God is true, because he is trustworthy in character, actions, and history. His character can be checked out. He keeps his promises, and they are good. He does not approve of everything that goes on in the real world. Instead, he sent his Son to redeem the world, and he will come again to judge it. We know that we live in a moral universe of right and wrong, rather than of mere power and weakness. Through Christ's death we have forgiveness. Through his resurrection we have hope. Birth and death—a cyclical normality in the flow of time—are not the only markings of human life.

This is so much more than what most people understand Christianity or faith in Christ to be! We live in a moral universe, not one controlled by fate or by an unfathomable will of God. There are personal choices to be made on the basis of good and sufficient reasons. We are not part of a collective, of an extended family or tribal tradition, when it comes to moral and personal responsibilities. God acts in history, not only in people's lives. God does not will all events. Therefore, we need to be discerning. There are personal sin and foolishness and a remedy in the work of Christ. Evil is a result of a mistaken view, of structural wrong, or of cultural patterns. And at some point there is always the individual choice to believe the truth or a lie about any aspect of reality.

In the Thessalonian passages there is an interesting focus on God, not on Christ. The Thessalonians turned to the Creator of the universe, the true and living God, by way of his Son. It gives us food for thought when we see the almost idolatrous focus on Jesus in much of contemporary, personalized Christianity, rather than on the Father, whose love sent Jesus to redeem us.

Paul praised the church for its total change from idols to the living God. A whole structure of information was involved. They saw life, all of it, from a different perspective. They were not simply given the name of Jesus and then told to discover their own definition for it. Their focus was not their own history, but the history of God in the world. There is something wonderfully objective and historical about this turn from idols, from the tribal to the true, which we have almost lost in our pursuit of personal truth, multicultural openness, and denominational fragmentation.

That realization of the living and accessible, the true and objective, led to a powerful change in their lives. Their faith, hope, and love were expressed in their work, labor, and endurance. We do not see this as a new and noble state of psychological development, but as a shift in their perspectives with very practical consequences.

In the second chapter Paul reminded the church in Thessalonica of the foundation for this change in worldview. He did not trick them (v. 3). What he told them was truthful in content. He did not flatter them (v. 5) or ask for payment. That same honesty also gave him the courage to speak when there was strong opposition (v. 2).

He reminded them of all the emotional and passionate ways in which he had lived among them. "Like a mother caring for her little children" (v. 7) is followed by his reminder that he toiled and suffered hardship to be like a brother to them (v. 9). Like "a father" (v. 11) he dealt with them to encourage them. Out of a concern for their lives and thoughts, Paul lived out among them all ranges of passionate, honest, caring relationships.

Yet with all this effort on the part of Paul, the real reason the church of Thessalonica believed a new perspective and began practicing a biblical ethic is that they "received the Word of God" (2:13). Paul told them, "You accepted it not as the word of men, but as it actually is, the Word of God, which is at work in you who believe" (2:13).

This is a refreshing focus on the word, or text, and not on Paul's personality. Their foundation was not the memory of a personality or a personal experience, which have become so central to our generation always in pursuit of another satisfying experience. The Thessalonians did not have certain passages in mind, but what God had said in all of Scripture; for while he was in Thessalonica, Paul had shown that this Jesus is the Christ.

Presenting a complete picture was characteristic for Paul's teaching. He wrote Romans to argue the case for the truth of the gospel against a host of possible objections. In Athens he taught that the unknown God could in fact be known by his word, his creation, and his historic work in Jesus Christ.

"Man does not live on bread alone but on every word that comes from the mouth of the Lord" (Deuteronomy 8:3). That Word is the foundation, the set of glasses that clarifies our understanding of life in the real world. It addresses our minds and nurtures our sensibilities to withstand the temptations of sensuality (Ephesians 4:17–19). The believers in Thessalonica (modern Salonica) had turned to God from idols because they found that the Word of God gives a better understanding of the real world than the word of men and women. Scripture is not based on a collection of human stories. It is not an explanation of how the world is to be embraced as normal.

The Word of God gives a broad framework for a moral stand in an immoral world.

To the end of the third chapter Paul praised the church for standing firm in persecution. Their neighbors had tried to kill Paul, and these neighbors would make them suffer as well (2:14). That should not surprise them, since the discovery of truth does not always please those for whom it is an admonition to change their ways. But the believers should not "be unsettled by these trials" (3:3). He told them that they would be persecuted (v. 4). And he was pleased to hear that they were "standing firm in the Lord" in spite of their hardship (v. 8).

The Bible never praises the status quo or calls people to submission under the dictates of normality. Religions tend to require that of their adherents. They link the individual experience to some supposed meaningful universal of nature, the will of God, or the cosmos. But God calls people to stand against the normality of suffering. We are not to accept it or even death. The Bible does not promise a good or easy life. More often than not, life is dangerous, difficult, and painful.

But we are promised real blessing and deliverance. The joy that the Bible speaks of is the joy of knowing that there is a moral God who will judge. That gives us confidence that we are not foolish when we complain about life in a fallen world. We need to remember the contrast with religions when we see the God of the Bible create a covenant with us, so that we don't have to merge with nature or the powers that be.

He is a moral God. He also weeps over the fall and its effects. He is not asleep when sin and death affect his creation. Jesus was furious at the tomb of Lazarus (John 11:33, 38). (The NIV says "deeply moved" and "troubled," but the Greek word ἐνεβριμησατο—aorist of ἐμβριμαομαι—means "to snort with fury.") He did not just weep tears of sorrow, but he had a gut-level reaction to his world having been spoiled. He who would moments later raise Lazarus from the dead was angry at death being present in his creation.

There is no other reason to believe God than that he is morally credible. The Word of God informs us of this fact against all present appearances of his absence. It is only a matter of time before everlasting righteousness will be brought in (Daniel 9:24). It is not a question of whether God's standards are different, whether he cares, or whether I am possibly mistaken when I don't approve of the status quo. The Word by which we are called to live confirms our anguish, justifies our cynicism, and responds with authority and beauty. The battle will be won not by us, not necessarily in our lifetime, but for sure. God will not abandon his creation to sin and the results of sin.

That is a radically different view of the world than what is found in religions of the world. It will change your perspective and your actions. It is not based on clever ideas. They would not suffice. It is based on what God has said and on what he has already done. The same God who ran after Adam rather than leaving him to the consequences of his choice is also the one who will solve the problem of what to do about a spoiled world.

With the worldview of the Bible, men and women are called to march to a different drummer. It will demand that we change our understanding, our choices, and our priorities. We should educate our minds and hearts to do so.

Changing a worldview is a frightening process for many people. Old patterns and beliefs are questioned and made relative. The solid structures of belief groups are broken up. It may set children against their parents, as Jesus warned. Often these structures are the only safety, offering a way to understand and approve the way life is. And yet, for the sake of human beings—their lives, their visions, and their future—faulty worldviews need to be changed. Where that does not take place, the old patterns with their destructive effects continue.

Anthropologists may not like this change in the way people think and live. The indigenous group is broken up and removed from further study. The pristine innocence seen in other groups is lost when those groups change their ways in light of the gospel. But then any sensitive person will have seen all along that what seemed pristine could only be called that by people from the outside. Inside the group the religious perspective had most frequently functioned like a prison for people on death row.

We will always have our own problems as a result of sin and disobedience. Therefore, we must not transpose our patterns without sensitivity. We must not absolutize our accomplishments. We are ourselves constantly in need of further instruction from God's Word. But all this does not add up to a rejection of the good things God has already worked in us in areas that transcend the personal and psychological.

Where God's Word has been used to establish an ethic of life, it has led to people being able to put food on the table, to care for the sick and to make them well, to struggle for better laws and relationships, as well as to protect their fragile existence from the ravages of a fallen nature. We must continue to take his Word as the basis for struggling against thorns and thistles by the sweat of the brow, against false information and poor kings, and against false priests and unjust judges. When teaching must be handed over to people apt to teach and faithful, not everyone of goodwill alone is indicated.

A change of worldview is not a philosophical discussion, an abstract consideration among many options. It is a turn from erroneous views about God and people to those that are factually and morally true.

6

Ethics in the Circle of Life

We know that Paul did not spend very much time in Thessalonica. In Acts 17 we are told that he was there only for the days between three weekends, and then a mob of jealous people drove him out of town. He had pointed out that the Bible read in their synagogue spoke of the Messiah coming in history. The person Jesus, who had lived and taught and was crucified and then rose from the dead in Israel during their own lifetime, was that Messiah. Paul had drawn for them a whole picture of understanding to explain the truth about Jesus. He had used prophecies from their own Scriptures as well as events in their own historic time to make his case.

He had distinguished the living and true God from Greek idols. He had explained the linear view of history from God's promise of a living future in contrast to the cyclical views of Greek culture. He had pointed to the risen Son of God to teach that there is eternal life in distinction to the Greek view that human beings are dead forever after. And he had pointed out to them that we live in a moral universe in which good and evil will be judged. Instead of people's lives being determined by an impersonal fate, there is a God whose wrath will judge all unrighteousness in history and who in love has provided Christ as atonement for us, once for all.

We notice at once that during those few days Paul had done more than teach about salvation. He had also instructed them in a biblical worldview. Just as Jesus was the Messiah in real history, there would be real consequences to the way they looked at and acted in their history. The Messiah was not an idea to be used to create positive attitudes about life. Since the Messiah had come, lived, and taught in real history, they had better change the way they lived in their own moments of history.

The Bible never talks about a different world from the one we live in. It does not draw us away from the context of reality into a spiritual dimension. It does not talk about believing certain things as doctrines or as part of a confession without showing the practical consequences, which should express what we believe. We are reminded to be not only hearers, but also doers (James 1:22).

Christians do not believe in a personal mystery religion, parallel to the Greek and Roman cults. Instead, we believe that the God of the Old Testament, faithful to his promises, revealed in real history the answer to our legal problem of guilt in the death of the Lamb of God. We also expect him to continue his work faithfully through Christ's resurrection until the Lord's physical reign on earth in righteousness as the Messiah. We are to follow in practice what we believe to be true, moral, and right.

This is not only a command to follow without question. It also corresponds to how we actually live. What we really believe is expressed by the choices we make in our lives. If we believe that certain mushrooms are poisonous, we will not eat them. Our actions and choices actually speak more clearly than our words, which can too easily be used to tell lies, to confuse, or to merely sound pleasing or religious.

The teachings of Paul always included instructions on how to practice the life of a Christian. Doctrine is not a set of phrases or a mark of identity or membership rules for an association. It is the summary statement about the way we understand reality: God, human beings, and life in the real world. Therefore, it is always exposed to the reality of human existence, where it can be examined to be reasonable, truthful, and fitting.

The Ten Commandments are not membership rules or moral trip wires to see whether we obey. They are foremost God's careful description of reality. They clarify what is true and right at a time of heightened "transgressions" (Galatians 3:19), when truth and justice are diluted or perverted. Our generation, with its moral and cultural relativism, would benefit from a similar affirmation of reality.

Reality needs clarification anytime that confusion or wild imagination or ideologies take over. The Ten Commandments inform us about the shape of the real world and wake us out of any discouragement and personal imaginings.

For these same reasons, Paul instructed the Thessalonians concerning practical aspects of their daily lives (1 Thessalonians 4:1). He did not leave them with just some general spiritual notions and encouragements about God and the age to come. His instruction was very specific, touching on expanding circles around the core of life. He began with the most intimate, personal, and immediate situation. Starting from the center he walked them to the periphery, where Christians make contact with their neighbors in society.

Before we examine Paul's teaching here, we need to acknowledge how normal it is to find instructions in the Bible. For many people exposed to our intellectual and spiritual climate, this may come as a surprise. A society as much in love with personal freedoms as ours finds it increasingly difficult to admit that we live in a world that already has definitions.

We have choices, but they are limited by what went on before (the raw material) as well as by the consequences that follow (we will have to eat the stew we cook). Our children will also judge us for the world we hand them. And finally we must stand before God the Creator.

In past generations Christians made many rules and expected conformity. Life in community requires that. Words like *police*, *politeness*, and *politics* describe what is necessary to function as a society in a city (Greek: *polis*), community, or state. Even though these rules often went beyond what the Bible directly states and were more cultural than final, Christians still operated within the recognition that we live in a defined world. At present a considerable reticence about giving direct instructions is developing among some Christians in reaction against the past. They fear that instructions control and influence their lives too much. They see instruction as an expression of arrogance by those who claim to know toward those who still learn. It is suggested that God's Spirit must do that teaching himself and that he would do it differently than we would. They replace information given by God to all of us with personal insight, personal stories, and existential convictions.

Hesitating before following instructions may be a healthy recognition of the limits of our present understanding. We need to be discerning and to refuse further ideological temptations, after having been frequently instructed by false authorities in our own lifetime. But I suspect that, often, hesitation is born out of either false humility or false spirituality. They constitute actually a kind of arrogance coupled to an intellectual and social laziness. "Who are we to teach others, since we ourselves are far from perfect?" some will ask. "We want to learn in community," others say. "We come to learn more than we come to teach" is often suggested. Yet Paul considered himself "the chief of sinners" and still taught.

In reaction to many religious people who draw attention in public to themselves, their experiences, and their popularity, we may hesitate from fear of appearing authoritarian. We shy away from giving too many detailed instructions about very central realms of human life in the real world. But we must avoid wrapping ourselves in a carpet of contradictions: We cannot say with certainty that we can't very well be certain about anything.

Such hesitation may reveal a wish to appear humble and spiritual in response to the growing mechanization and regimentation of life. A hunger for spirituality is understandable and even desirable. We are not machines. There is a life of the spirit. Whenever either science or government has tried to reduce people to mathematical parameters, the human being turns inward to discover something genuine and free. That discovery can be thoughts or religious experiences. It can be an idea of life and beauty or a sensation of warmth and humanity. In much of the former Soviet Union (but also increasingly in our own societies), people search for spirituality in music, folk customs, and religious practices. Antimaterialism, anti-intellectualism, and an embrace of feeling, traditions, and community characterize spirituality in this vein.

This is hardly biblical spirituality, but its opposite. It is a movement away from content and certainty. It embraces elements of our more recent anti-intellectual history after the large-scale rejection of biblical Christianity as a foundation for all of life and culture.

In more recent intellectual history it has become acceptable not to have a position, since all reality is believed to be only a series of personal impressions and experiences. We may show how something worked "in my life," forgetting that God has said certain things quite definitely about his definite creation. There are Ten Commandments, which are not Ten Suggestions. God wrote them in stone; they are not community expectations as formulated by Moses after a lonely mountaintop experience and then often rejected by an obstinate people.

Our whole culture is also obstinate. More than that, it has even abandoned the notion of objective truth. The artist today reveals a searching process, rather than giving a courageous, superior vision of an objective reality. And subject to the idea of cultural relativism, the biblical text itself is reduced to what it might have meant to the original hearers in their changing cultural context. The original intent is understood to be shaped and limited by the author's relationship to the original hearers. We can learn, at best, by analogy from it, but not from insight into a common human quest.

The notion that God has something to say to the whole human race is weakened when we focus primarily on what we personally get out of a text. I am, of course, addressed as a significant member of that human race. But we should not view the text simply in light of what it might say to me in my current personal need. Biblical spirituality reveals the source of our wisdom and addresses us with real content about all areas of life. There is a God whose Spirit reveals to our minds and hearts what is the truth of the universe. The Bible gives theological, intellectual, physical, and metaphysical answers to some of the most urgent questions of the human race. But that option is denied when everything is strained through my changing set of needs. Some of the meat may never reach me and thus never satisfy my hunger.

Outside the realm addressed by the words of the Bible lies the modern separation in people's minds between evangelism and discipleship. In this model, evangelism presents the choice for salvation to the person, and discipleship deals with the life of the Christian in sanctification. There is a certain logical sequence or even progression in this model. But any evangelistic effort needs to explain enough of the full counsel of the Bible *before* a person becomes a Christian. Evangelism without this fuller explanation appeals only on the level of

Ethics in the Circle of Life

emotions and personal need and does not help a person consider whether he or she would want to believe in God, who has specific ethical standards and expectations.

This division between evangelism and discipleship makes much of the "love of God," while diminishing the specific character and holiness of God. This is an unwarranted distinction. There is no way to become a Christian without accepting Christ as Lord over all of life, thought, and practice.

Paul saw his teaching as a whole. There is no evidence of separate compartments in his thinking. He told his listeners who God is, what he has done on our behalf, and what is involved in believing: repeated existential choices to do what is right in the objective, fallen world. Both the Old Testament and the New Testament state that love for God is expressed through keeping his commandments. In this sense Noah was a righteous man, as were Job and many others praised in the Bible for their right thoughts and actions. Paul gave the believers in Thessalonica a body of insights, not bits and pieces of pious admonitions about love, hope, and faith or a bundle of legalistic prescriptions. His mind did not work that way. We find a unity of teaching reflected in all of Paul's epistles.

This understanding about the relationship between the truth of the Bible and the truth of the real world also characterizes his work as described in the book of Acts. The apostle preached, argued, expounded, set forth, explained, refuted, and discussed. A picture of open and honest communication emerges in which people are shown the wholeness of the gospel. A worldview comes together in opposition to other worldviews. Neither the Aristotelian concern with nature nor the Platonic concern with universals, ideals, and the soul comes together in a similar fashion, for each view lacks an important slice of reality. Becoming a Christian has something to do with erasing files from the hard drives of our brains when their contents no longer explain the real world.

Paul instructed because there is a reality to be explained. He did not perform, blend, glow, or grin Buddha-like. Reality demands an explanation, not a smoothing over or a denial. Paul could make a case, not just hold an opinion persuasively. He did not see his work in contradiction to or replacing the work of the Holy Spirit. Rather, since the Holy Spirit had already given the Old Testament and its explanations about much of life, Paul could explain spiritual things to the people intelligently.

A refusal to teach and to inform often sounds more spiritual. It comes across more as a softer approach than confronting or hurting people. But it may often hide a lack of clear understanding in the teacher. We forget that God's Spirit works with the minds we have and desires to educate them. He wants us to know more and different things. In a dangerous world we need more, not less, discernment.

That same Spirit has already said quite a few things in the Word (of which he is the author) to all of us before we ever get to consider what else he might want to say to us personally. In fact, only a critical and informed mind is able to recognize when additional insight is from God's Spirit. Without Scripture informing the mind, many people take their own flights of fantasy to be instructions from the Spirit. Lacking basic means of control and examination, people become much more vulnerable to weird spiritual sources.

The Bible starts with the word, with language and information. It does not contrast or replace these with vague "spiritual" knowledge. Spiritual knowledge, according to Jewish thought and Christianity, is not "Platonism with Jesus." Rather, it is the content and understanding that God's Spirit tells our trained spirits (1 Corinthians 2:6–16). That training is based on seeking to understand the Word of God. (*How Does a Poem Mean?* by John Ciardi and Miller Williams and *How to Read a Book* by Mortimer J. Adler and Charles Van Doren are helpful tools in figuring out how to understand any writing, including the Bible.)

Tragically, the trust in the Spirit's work is often not matched with the need to train our listening faculties. Much of the search for spiritual teaching is closer to magic than to biblical instruction. As for Paul, he was not so inclined. He instructed the people about some very specific things. In matters touching family relations, neighborly attitudes, the wider civic realities, and the approach to a tragic life, he instructed with such conviction that some might call it arrogance. He understood that this instruction was not a matter of a richer personal opinion or goodwill, but of certain expectations, of clear thinking, and of courage that would serve as a foundation for a radically different worldview. This is not the vision of a different world, but a different view of the seen and unseen world that exists with us as a part of it. The Creator informs the biblical view of the world. It links attitudes and specific behavior to what was created from the beginning. It is not merely an effort by the wise to create a smoothly running society. Peace in the city was *a*, but not *the*, major goal. Against the constant exposure to sin and the tendency to chaos, the Bible calls us to constructive intervention on behalf of human beings.

From Paul's teachings in the fourth chapter of 1 Thessalonians, we understand that the first circle of life drawn around us (vv. 3–8) contains the innermost realities in our existence. Here we stand at the center of all human life. We are born into a family. One certain man is our father; we have only one biological mother. Others may take care of us, but each of us is the child of one specific relationship. This must remain clear, unique, and precious. The ethic of the family goes all the way back to God creating humans male and female in a mutually dependent and beneficial relationship.

Both are made in the image of God. There is no room for a lower view of one by the other. "Your desire will be for your husband, and he will rule over you" (Genesis 3:16) was

Ethics in the Circle of Life

stated as a tragic realization in a fallen world. It is a part of fallen human reality, not a command on how to structure a relationship. Every man is born from a woman. That most intimate relationship between a man and a woman continues something of the relationships among the persons of the triune Godhead. In that relationship between equals, language, meaning, love, trust, and loyalty are discovered, promised, and practiced. Here exist privacy, incomparable intimacy, and uniqueness between two people for a lifetime. Here the first wounds of a broken humanity are discovered and forgiveness is experienced. Here we can cry without having to be ashamed or being ridiculed.

For these reasons there should be no break in any area of this unique relationship. We need to train ourselves in self-control, make wise choices, and prepare ourselves to deliberately reject very real distractions. We were created sexual beings, but sexuality as passionate lust can smash the intimacy of our marriage commitment. It is common to be attracted to alternative relationships, but by making choices we confirm that we are not driven by lust but choose to love. We are choice makers, not victims of instincts, natural possibilities, or rich imaginations.

Sexual immorality must be avoided if we are to honor the neighbor and not take advantage of him or her. To become intimate with a second person kills the commitment to the first. It also deceives the second about the freedom to make a new commitment. A promise to love can never be a temporary arrangement. Love by its definition is an enduring promise, not a series of events. I create a new situation through a loving commitment with lasting consequences. It cannot be terminated at will.

Just as we are born to a man and a woman who remain our parents forever, they should remain husband and wife. Where that relationship depends on likes and dislikes or on moments rather than commitment, love becomes sex, loyalty becomes a farce, and trust is always violated. Marriage is then no longer sanctified. God had something else in mind when he made us male and female and created an interdependence between a husband and wife. Outside of this we lower ourselves to be driven by base reactions, by passionate lust like those people who model their actions on natural drives found in impersonal nature.

The second circle indicated in our passage encloses those outside the marriage commitment (1 Thessalonians 4:9–10). "Brotherly love" realizes the social context of all of life. We are not isolated. Our life consists of more than free-floating atoms. We are neighbors to our neighbors and brothers and sisters to each other. We are individuals, but not individualists. We live in a social context in which we are more like each other than like anything else in nature. We may not easily enjoy a certain person for a variety of reasons, and we may even need a door to limit someone's access to us. We are not even called to like all people. That would require a certain *like-ness* beyond our being human beings together. In the real world we think and react differently, have different sensitivities, like different music, and eat different foods.

But we are to love others. We are even called to love our enemy. Fundamental to this command is the awareness of the unity of the human race. We are created from the same set of parents and did not evolve at different times by accident. After the fall, things and people changed. Human existence has become extremely fragile. There is now much tragedy in our lives. We are threatened and defend ourselves. We are in many areas incapable of surviving without the help of others.

Whereas Darwin taught that nature unfolds a battle for the survival of the fittest and thus eliminates the weak genes, the Bible teaches that we must love one another, for not one human being should be left to extermination. Nature is amoral. It functions according to mechanics. Nature does not shed tears. But people are different. We survive by our trained minds, not our biology. And we should work to have our neighbors survive, because we should love them more than an abstract idea about humanity or people in general. Missing that focus, all kinds of humanistic ideologies such as Marxism and Fascism, China's great leap forward, and Pol Pot's national purification eliminated in recent years millions of individuals in pursuit of a vision of a better humanity.

Again, the biblical ethic is one that confirms that we are people, not pawns in a cosmic theater. Unless we obey the command to love, the animal in us will be let loose and dominate. Personal survival by the elimination of competition will become the principle manner of relating to others.

Love does not mean approving everything that another person chooses. It does mean having deep compassion in the midst of the tragedy of human life in a fallen world. Love reaches out, builds bridges, and is gracious rather than demanding. Love does not take revenge, but forgives when forgiveness is asked for. In love we seek to understand the complexity of each situation and to avoid quick, superficial reactions. Love protects and corrects. Love enables us to empathize with those in need, because we take the time to imagine what their need might feel like.

Love also confronts, corrects, and critiques. It does not overlook the foolishness of others, but helps them to change their ways. It does not approve or neglect merely to avoid tension. It uses the tension to resolve conflict by getting to the heart of a dividing matter.

Human beings can love each other. Animals display protective instincts and what only to us as human beings *seems* to be love. For love is a choice, a creation, which does not always come naturally or easily. It is a learned response, not an instinctual one. By loving we prove to ourselves our distinct nature as people. It is an unending effort. Each day presents

Ethics in the Circle of Life

us with renewed choices: "We urge you, brothers, to do so more and more" (v. 10).

The third circle of life covered in Paul's instruction is the world beyond. It is the realm of human activities, of work, and of public responsibilities. It deals with us as human beings in a real world (vv. 11–12). Paul instructed the Thessalonians to work in order to live in the city. The specifics are in a sense incidental, but they serve us in understanding the biblical ethic for a normal life.

Paul instructed them to lead a quiet life. This does not refer to a submissive or hidden existence. This is not a call to be indifferent or to be a pushover. Paul himself did not teach in a corner or under cover of secrecy. He openly went to the synagogues and spoke in the markets. He argued, expounded, refuted, taught, reasoned, and lectured in public. But his manner was orderly, his arguments factual, and his sources were historical. "Quiet" stands in contrast to riotous, not to public or loud. Christians may cause riots by what they teach, but riots are the response of those who have nothing better to say, who fail to argue with the same sources, or who are mad from fear and hurt.

In Thessalonica itself the response to Paul had been a riot, which was caused by the jealousy of some Jews. They could not refute his argument, and this made them angry. They called a mob together (Acts 17:5) because they thought a crowd would intimidate him. But Paul had proved from their own Hebrew text that the historic person Jesus must be the Christ. Riots should not mark our lives. We should seek peace, love, truth, and freedom. But we do not purchase the respect of others by being silent, compliant, or indifferent.

We mind our own business (1 Thessalonians 4:11) when we struggle to live truthfully. We do not plant or follow gossip or false accusations. We do not make pronouncements in areas where real freedom is advocated. We do not legislate morality where the Bible is silent and where variety is the spice of life. We allow ourselves to be surprised by others where God's Word gives room for real creativity. We give advice when asked and do not interfere where people must make their own choices. This applies to all the areas of life where morality is not at play: areas of personal taste, of private imagination, and of unique personalities. We strive to distinguish central issues of truth from peripheral issues of taste and preference. Where God has not given specific instruction, we believe he has done so deliberately. The silences of Scripture are also inspired. And we mind our own business.

The admonition to work with our own hands affirms the nobility of work. It does not advocate manual over intellectual work but encourages work as a means of earning a living to avoid becoming a burden on others through dependency. This admonition is rooted in a number of aspects in the biblical view of life.

First, it reminds us that we live in a material world as

image bearers of the Creator. He worked for six days, making choices and forming all there is in its original existence. We continue that activity by our work. Adam worked before the fall. Work is not a curse, but a means of expressing personality, choice, and creativity. It has continued after the fall, even though under more difficult circumstances. Our understanding of the nobility of work is fundamental. It is part of the creation mandate in Genesis.

Second, we should live here on earth and not imagine being somewhere else. It is not a mark of spirituality to live off other people's work, like a parasite on a tree, while merrily pursuing loftier ideas. In the real world created by God for our existence, there are outcomes to effort and to neglect. Without effort there will be no benefit. Those who do not work should not eat. We do not live by miracles, but by fulfilling the mandate to work. Working with hands and mind is not a waste of time when we seek wisdom, righteousness, and a good life. Instead, we shape time through work. To be creative is the mark of human existence in the real world. Paul made tents and taught. All the parables of Christ have normal people working as their context. Spirituality has something to do with a relationship with the Creator, not with being independent from our bodies or from the world of time and space and things.

This wisdom needed a repeated reminder in Thessalonica. In the second letter (2 Thessalonians 3:10–12) Paul came back to it. There were people who in their own eyes were so close to God that they had stopped working. In the early church the influence of the Platonic tradition was often knocking on the door of biblical faith as Gnosticism. When it was allowed to enter, it encouraged people to sit on pillars in the desert or dwell in caves as hermits. There they prayed, closer to heaven and with as little contact with earth as possible. They saw matter as something evil and effort in nonspiritual matters as something mundane. But the Bible has saints working with their hands.

Third, work confirms to us our own importance and significance. Here we show to ourselves and to others that we matter. Without our effort, nature would be left to its amoral and mechanical self. Only by making an effort do we work against and affect the abnormality of the world. By work we show what we believe. By work we show that we love in deed.

Fourth, our work is necessary but does not identify us. There is no greater nobility to clean work than work that gets us dirty. Ideas and skill must come together to accomplish good things. We have our identity in being people made in God's image. We do not receive it from the type of work we do. Our value lies in being human, not in what we accomplish or how others judge us. We *are* people in God's image from the beginning and do not go through a process of *becoming* that.

The fourth circle of life acknowledges the basic tragedy of life after the fall. We grieve, but not as those who have no hope (1 Thessalonians 4:13). Answering what must have been a specific question concerning those who die before the return of Christ, Paul informed them about what will happen in the future. The time is unknown to us, but not the certainty of the future event.

This fourth circle clarifies a number of concerns beyond the immediate questions that are crucial to most people: questions about the absurdity of death, about the unfairness of all life, and about the tragedy of interrupted relationships. Paul's answers here are repeated in different places of the Bible. The Bible always encourages us to see life in the fallen world as a real tragedy, over which we are free—or even obliged—to grieve, but not as those "who have no hope."

Death is the last enemy to be abolished at the return of Christ (1 Corinthians 15). Until then it is the common tragedy, a brutal interruption of all we strive for from birth forward: life, relationships, continuity, and justice. We grieve because of death's power to break up what God made to be together. We grieve because of death's constant reminder of the fall in what was once God's perfect world.

We grieve because Christ grieved, moved with compassion and expressing anger, even though he would raise dead Lazarus a few moments later (John 11:33–44). We grieve because of all the sadness that death produces in the lives of others. We also grieve because the effects of the fall are on all components that make up human existence. The dust of death covers them all. Our health is imperfect, our relationships are wounded, our soul is heavy, and the world around us is spoiled. The lamb does not lie down with the lion. Thorns and thistles take over the fields. Genesis 3 is the beginning of human life as we now know it. And since that time there has been little change in its essential predicament.

Yet we do not grieve as those "who have no hope"! That hope refers to and encloses a future dimension when all things will be restored. From this certainty of a better future, we find strength to accept the present mandate to diminish the effects of the fall by human effort. The fall and its consequences, including death, should not define us. That we shall die is not the only certainty about us. Christ came into the world, died, and was raised in a real body. Death will not even be an inevitable experience forever, since one generation of people will see Christ and his victory in their lifetime.

Therefore, we make every effort to resist evil and the results of the fall. We work against a wounded nature, when the protection or repair of human life requires it. We are concerned about species threatened with extinction. We visit the doctor to get well. We exercise dominion to struggle for every ounce of life as an expression that God has created life and will re-create it. We heal patients even if only for a while as a moral statement to remind ourselves that there will be a resurrection at the return of Christ. There are no failed efforts. We are not running against windmills, but defying fate and resignation.

Others resign themselves to the inevitable, the seemingly natural, the end of life, and the nothingness beyond. We Jews and Christians raise our fists in defiance, and because something will be accomplished, this is not stupid. We do that and work because Christ will come again and bring real righteousness into our historic continuity with the resurrection from the dead. We have hope that in history the substance of renewal will come by a work of God, of which our efforts now are real shadows. While our work is like the firstfruits of a field, Jesus Christ at his coming will bring in the full harvest.

7

Gutsy Christians

With the hope of Christ's return in real history, we might want to throw all caution to the wind. Our hope is not a psychological attitude or wishful thinking, but the expectation of a certain historical reality. In light of a sure future in Christ's promises and the power of God, it would be easy to conclude that present efforts have little value. A similar temptation exists when a job is guaranteed and more preparation or present efforts are not required. When no value is placed on work itself and a certain outcome is guaranteed, human effort will diminish. In Eastern Europe seventy years of socialism produced the proverb "We pretend to work and they pretend to pay us." It is easy to slide into something like a midlife slowdown. A major slump often occurs after we have been accepted into a university or found our first employment. Does it really matter what we do when the outcome, good or bad, is fixed?

People may think that everything is fixed in concrete or written in stone when a promise is given, a document is signed, and tomorrow will come with certainty. Like a film in the can, their future is already locked in place. They forget that their own actions and behaviors still affect the world around them. But even when the anticipated events come to pass in history, the people themselves may be left standing outside or be swept aside by events in that history.

It happened to King Solomon. His father, David, had received an unconditional promise that the Messiah would come through his line. But the next generation, his son Solomon, had received the same promise, but conditionally. If Solomon would continue to believe and act as his father had done, then the future would arrive as announced. But if the condition were not fulfilled, history would be very different.

Solomon did not fulfill the condition. He went his own way, as we know. For political and personal reasons he did not continue faithfully in the ways of God. The consequence was that, while the promise of a certain future stood firm, the Messiah did not come through his family's line, but through the line of his brother Nathan. Solomon lost his participation in the working out of historic promises concerning the Messiah.

Gutsy Christians

The church of Thessalonica must have had some members who expressed the same underlying confusion in their response to Paul's teaching. They reasoned that if Christ is coming back, why continue the struggle to live as normal human beings. Let us just love and share and wait.

This is a very human reaction when we are stretched between the present struggle and its certain future resolution. We wonder what the point of the present exercise is. A purpose in life now involving much effort, work, and sweat is easily denied. Instead, and often under the guise of spirituality, the attitude changes and ideas about a different, more ideal world are embraced and advocated. We saw that in political ideologies under the wider influence of the Enlightenment.

The Enlightenment insisted on shedding light on what is true, seeking to know things for sure. People measured, counted, and weighed the world around them. They dismissed superstition and unfounded dogmas. They rightly believed that there is a real and rational world to be studied and to be known. In this way they were the true children of the Protestant Reformation over against blind dogmatism and plenty of myths in the Roman Church and pagan superstitions.

However, this rightful confidence in the logic of reality quickly turned into overconfidence. Nature could be measured in its forms, functions, and rationality. Nature, including human biology, was like a beautiful machine. It was then assumed that human beings would, in every area of their existence, want to function like a machine and in this way become rational and good and refined. What was discovered in biology as a hard science was soon proposed in sociology and psychology as soft sciences.

Initially the insistence on fact and reason recognized human personality, creativity, and choice. A broad awakening of human responsibility in all areas of life broke the fetters of earlier feudal structures, fatalism, and blind faith in life totally controlled by God, the church, or some other view of fate. But then the belief that human beings are part of the machinery again abandoned both reason and reference to facts, because such a view leaves out a person's *creativity* for both good and evil. It is a view some advocates *wished* to believe, regardless of factual observations of real human significance. After all the concern about reality rather than myth, the Enlightenment then produced its own kind of myth about reality, regardless of any concrete exigencies of human history, economics, and social/cultural morality.

Wishful thinking, make-believe, and grandiose schemes for the improvement of human nature became first encouraged and then widely accepted. They contained superior visions, for which the problems of the past should be put aside by enforced changes in the nature of human beings. Secular humanism, nationalism, fascism, and Marxism are all Enlightenment ideals. Yet their projected aims could only be pursued through violence to what is central in the real world, the human being. They each produced horribly destructive results in the real world.

The Bible always brings us back to the reality of the world, created and now fallen. There, human beings exist and have their being. The Bible's interest in dealing with the real world (rather than with a desirable but imaginary world) makes it a book about reality, not about fantasy, myths, and dreams. In the Bible's light, life becomes possible in a fallen world. The light of the Bible shines on the shape of reality, whereas the Enlightenment's views express wishful thinking and dreams from which we awaken into a life without a solution.

Paul continued his instruction about a Christian worldview in 1 Thessalonians 5 by placing much weight on the importance of living rather than on waiting for something else. In this and other letters he often anticipated and rejected the temptations of a Gnostic escape, which denies the reality of God's interest in the material and historic world. Paul denied all false spirituality, which, under a pretense of temperance, advocates abstinence from life, work, and responsibilities. Instead, he spoke of virtue and discipline in life so that we would know how far and where to go with anything we do. Paul's emphasis is not on hidden knowledge, secret ways, and mystic rules of behavior, but on discernment, light, and courage to live as God's creatures in the real world of history as real people.

It is often quite hard to keep the correct biblical focus. Some people tell us to fit in as part of society; others call us to keep our distance from the normal things of life. Both appeals, in fact, demonstrate that we are not fully comfortable with the status quo. This discomfort is a good view to have, for to be satisfied is to deny one of two things: (1) that there are problems in the real world or (2) that we should have moral and emotional reactions when we are exposed to the real world.

Buddha's teaching illustrates the opposite mentality. Buddhism solves the problem of moral and existential frustration by teaching steps toward detachment from reality in order to lose the awareness of real problems. On the other extreme, scientific naturalism suggests that all events are natural or facts without a moral component. There is nothing unnatural about events in nature, including human nature! Both Buddhism and naturalism suggest that problems lie in our perception and, therefore, that *the way we see* things is what needs to be changed.

Some Christians suggest a similar approach without realizing that it dilutes our being in the image of God in all of life. When they are dreaming about becoming something other than human beings, they separate from either the reality of the world or the reality of necessary moral judgment. Yet we cannot live in a better world of our imagination. Instead, we are much more in line with a biblical view when we impose discipline on what we are and do not pursue what we wish to be but can never achieve.

There are unavoidable givens in reality. They are historical and have their creational definitions. Adjustments can and must be made in our moral attitudes and realistic practice, not in seeking to deny reality by becoming someone else or some other creature, like an angel. This pursuit of being someone other than who we actually are is widespread in our culture, which enables and encourages us to seek to be elsewhere, richer, younger, married to someone else and living on the opposite coast, or away from it all in, for example, Taos or the Idaho panhandle.

The pursuit of living elsewhere as someone else robs us of ever being able to actually live. We run after the next thing and have little time or patience to live now, here, and with ourselves. This is more than having a rich imagination. It expresses nervousness about being; boredom about place, work, and personality; and a deep disturbance about our gender, age, physical shape, and personality. Our culture may prolifically produce books about living and yet miss the experience of actual life for lack of time and pleasure. Often we work so much to be able to finance a relationship with our children that we miss actually spending time with them. We work in expectation of a promotion rather than enjoying the work we do now. We train for a future possibility and miss the one at our fingertips. We are encouraged to pursue a future career and stumble over the shards of our broken marriage on the path. Our historical experience, when our forebears moved west not so much to have land but just to be on the move, may have set a regrettable pattern.

Always on the move are those among us who place no weight and respect on living now, because they have higher ideals. They think perhaps that the normal things of human life are temporary and therefore a waste—they, too, will pass away. Such people neglect the common things of creation in order to take time for more "spiritual" things. The mistake is to divide life into compartments and our work into our job and our calling. Such divisions are not biblical. They reveal a Platonic influence in our thinking. The Gnostic heresy was always a lure in the early church—and Paul spoke, wrote, and lived against this way of thinking. Platonism, when incorporated into Gnosticism, will encourage an impoverished and suspicious relationship to matter. In contrast to this, the biblical view starts with creation. Salvation enters only after guilt has been acknowledged. The material and daily world is the stage for all of life. The human dilemma is moral, not metaphysical. There is no mistake; nothing is merely temporary to our being human beings with body and soul. Christ came to earth and confirmed its rightful existence. Our place for human life is not in heaven. We are neither a mistake nor a temporary apparition. We do not seek another form of existence, that is, of angels or spirits, but life on earth in the full presence of God. The New Jerusalem will come down to a restored earth. That is the reason why the expectation of the resurrection is so central to biblical teaching.

Both Christians and secular people often exhibit a disregard for the real and justify it with their focus on goals. The present reality is valued less than the imagined future. Christians tend to deny the real from a spiritual interest while people with a secular focus deny it because their hearts and minds are centered on what they hope to accomplish one day. Both run away from the reality of the now, pursuing in the "not yet" a better, though always abstract, goal. Both favor the idea over the real, an impression given others over the concrete abilities and tasks at hand.

There is no justification for neglecting our life, work, or family and justifying it from some supposed spiritual concern. Our homes should reveal more of real human life lived in them than give an impression of the financial power of the owners. Our music should surround our conversations, not replace them. Noise of undefined origin and purpose is no substitute for deliberate compositions that express mood, tension, pleasure, surprise, and variation. What is communicated and how it is done is of greater importance than the potency of expensive sound systems.

In many areas we get by with pretending, or as Boorstin suggests, with an image rather than the substance because we think real life is somewhere else or will occur at a later time.[1] What is called "materialism," because it involves things constantly bought and traded as an activity, is actually a kind of antimaterialism, because the objects are not really valued in themselves. They merely serve the purpose of making the owner feel more important, richer, and more adjusted to modern demands. They are not as much owned as they are consumed. Being "in" and giving an appearance of respectability without knowing what being human involves are signs of cynicism and despair, rather than of wholeness and contentment.

Gnosticism, which we associate with a mindset of the first century, is also among us today, though the external particulars would of course be quite different. In this view, real life is understood to take place elsewhere. It is accessible only to the initiated, who feel they are in touch with the personal divine. Judaism and Christianity, by contrast, affirm that we are meant to live as human beings in time and space in a real world with our minds trained and sharpened. We work with our minds and hands to do what is right and good.

To combat the Gnostic temptation in any age, Paul told believers that the time of Christ's return is unknown to us. We can count on it, but we have no knowledge of the specific time. Jesus will come again, like a thief in the night. No date

---

1 Daniel Boorstin, *The Image: A Guide to Pseudoevents in America* (New York: Harper, 1961).

is fixed (1 Thessalonians 5:1–3). Christians should not wish to get out of reality, but to transform it into righteousness. We grieve over imperfections, not over life itself or humanity or necessary effort.

Therefore, life at present is already intrinsically meaningful for the Christian and the Jew. It is the only life we have. We are not waiting to receive life at some later moment. This is it: here and now and without end. So we are to enjoy it as meaningful now because nothing else will be added to give us meaning. There will be a renewal; there will be righteousness and justice. There will be God's kingdom on earth in which his will is fully done. Having eternal life through faith in Christ means that our life now will not be destroyed by death. It does not mean that this life is merely a holding pattern until we land somewhere more real. The additions and changes in the future will not make our life important only then. It already is that by virtue of God having created us to be significant human beings from the beginning.

We know there is a future Sabbath rest (Hebrews 4). Each Sabbath now is to be a slice from that future hope. Jews celebrate the Sabbath as a day on which they can taste most realistically something of what life shall be in the presence of the Messiah. The Jew experiences on the Sabbath something of what human life was meant to be all along. It is a day of greater freedom from the fallen world and its necessities, a day of celebration, of study, and of arguments for the sake of

God. You put on your best clothes, a table is laid for a feast, and you study and enjoy God's Word and work in creation. The promised rest does not encompass idleness or some form of Breughel's "Schlaraffia," a land of plenty where chickens fly through the air already roasted. Instead, I understand it as an eternity of work and accomplishments without the disturbances of frustration, failure, and finally death in any of its ugly manifestations.

Our life at all times ought to reflect this view of human existence. We are not to go through life with our senses dulled as if we were asleep, but with our senses alert and self-controlled (1 Thessalonians 5:6). Since we are not dead but alive, we should live together with God here and now (v. 10). We should be able to include him in our work and share with him our mealtimes, our games, and our conversations. Can you take him to your Christian bookstore, or would that be embarrassing? It is often so for me, since many of them have few books and much Christian kitsch. The items for sale inform less about God and human beings in the real world than console and distract people with the appearance of spiritual interests. It is all about packaging, and very little concerns the content of what we believe.

Would you want God to come to your Christian women's club meeting to add a few words after the advertised talk on gardening or outdoor cooking or cosmetics? I realize that some things are "cultural," but how do they fit into a biblical worldview? Does "truth in labeling" legislation not apply to Christian things as well?

Do we argue for the sake of heaven or for the sake of power? Do we struggle to be real human beings, created in God's image? Do we study historical criteria for art? Have we thought about what a person needs to know of skills and content to be considered an educated person? What are the marks of a civilization? What is tragedy in the eyes of God? Do we know where to go to reeducate our minds and to sensitize and educate our consciences for better service? Do we know how to be more alert and self-controlled instead of being driven by circumstances and living without a moral compass?

We are told in the Bible to always be on our guard. We live in a world with clear distinctions from the outset. Water is not land, light is not darkness, the human being is not an animal, and creation is not God. Consequently, we need to discern in all areas between what is right and good and what is not. After the entrance of sin and confusion, this is no pretty or easy world. We are no longer in the garden of Eden, and we are not yet in Christ's kingdom. We are on our guard when we have learned from our mistakes and from generous instructions from knowledgeable and wise people. But let us also be more alert when it comes to the kind of concerns and situations the Bible talks about. As light we should illumine the darkness, remove the shadows, and speak from greater discernment. It takes that to be wiser and more knowledgeable. Knowing human nature from sharing in it rather than as a doctrinal position, we should be more aware of both the greatness and the tragedy found in each member of the human race—ourselves and our neighbors. In this fallen world, there are real specks of dust and real beams in our eyes.

We should admire work done well and, at the same time, not be distraught when people cheat, lie, and break promises. To be spiritual does not mean having no interest in material things, forsaking good training, or refusing to develop skills. God created a material world in which he delights and will redeem. We should know it, enjoy it, and make good use of it. We are given dominion and must recognize and diminish uninformed, selfish domination as much as fatalistic submission. We should be interested in ways to have moral dominion through the study of medicine, economics, and marketing as well as through the study of the destructive results of consumerism. Spiritual people are not against a material reality. They work with it from a mindset of what morally *should be*, not only what materially *can be*.

Spirituality does not mean to be mindless, submissive, and resigned. We need discernment to understand spiritual and intellectual ideas and their power in the hearts and minds of people. The problem is an untrained mind, not the mind itself. The mind needs to be sensitized, educated, and informed. We are encouraged to seek wisdom and the ability to observe, to weigh, and to anticipate. By gathering the pieces of knowledge, we are better able to choose what is wise, wholesome, and beneficial. As spiritual people we must listen to God's words about all of life in the midst of God's work in creation. Both will inform us, encourage us, and make us more human, just, and kind.

Spiritual people desire to understand the Creator's purposes, not to escape from creation into another state of being. Drugs will do that because they distort reality. God's Spirit, by contrast, will make reality more comprehensible. Paul warned believers against being drunk with wine because that distorts reality and reactions. Instead, we should be filled with the Spirit (Ephesians 5:18), which leads to greater and more sensitive discernment.

Being spiritual does not mean feeling good, experiencing happiness, or being untroubled by the state of the world around us. To remain unaffected by the suffering of soul and body in the people around us is not spirituality, but insensitivity. Jesus wept over Jerusalem, pleaded with people, and grieved for those who suffered. While Herod had the Baptist beheaded at his feast, Jesus fed the five thousand and told them how to live. He agonized and then changed the situation he faced. He was the man of sorrows, not the model for a happy life. We neither seek nor avoid pain as a priority of spirituality. In a fallen world, the barometer of our well-being is not found in numbers or in our feeling good or positive. God defines what is good, regardless of our feelings about a situation at a certain moment.

Being spiritual has to do with understanding and following God's Word. Spiritually obedient people warn those who are idle. They encourage the timid, help the weak, and are patient (1 Thessalonians 5:14). We should be recognized by our kindness, which is not the same as indifference. Kindness gives approval easily, but never without reason. Kindness makes others comfortable, but never pretends or covers up. Kindness includes the compassionate reproach, the warning before danger, walking the extra mile, and stating boundaries. Kindness is involved when a teacher gives a fitting grade to point out weaknesses and when merchandise of poor quality is taken off the shelf.

The Christian is to be joyful always (v. 16). In our age, with its focus on how we feel more than on how we are, we may miss the real and deep joy that comes from knowing that we do not live in an insane, immoral world without resolution. Joy is not a permanent grin on the face or a shallow pleasure that overlooks the tragedy of life. An injured child, a broken friendship, a frustrated effort, an unfinished conversation, even a loss of childhood or reduced abilities as we grow old are examples of tragic situations. We rejoice in what can be done while we grieve over the pain that an imperfect world inflicts.

When we bring all of life's situations and discoveries to God as we talk and walk, we fulfill the command to always pray (v. 17). This is no invitation to a flight from the world.

The monastic withdrawal or an analogy to Jesus' fasting for forty days is not a biblical rule. The vow of silence to the world is not the same as constant prayer. We pray to a specific God as specific people in a specific world that God created and in which he became man. There are not two worlds—one spiritual and of grace and the other of necessity related to work, thought, and time.

Instead, we acknowledge consciously God's existence, his power, his being, and his character; and we are thankful. When I tighten a bolt, I thank God for a regular universe, for real matter, and for minds that can analyze, invent, and figure out ways to make life easier. I thank God for tools and for a job that I can get done. When I listen to a piece of music, I marvel at the original choice in the Trinity to create human beings. I marvel at the musician who trained hard to play well. I marvel at creativity, dominion, minds, and hands. I am intrigued by the different language, grammar, and meaning contained in music I listen to with my ears and my emotions. All this is prayer, adoration, thankfulness, and petition.

We give thanks (v. 18) for God's character at all times. Above all presently good or absurd situations, he exists and has spoken. He comforts and sheds light on how to cope with all situations, whether to work with them or against them. Not all events that happen are to be accepted. Where God grieves, I am called to join the battle. I am not alone. I am also not free to merely recognize and enjoy my feelings. In a fallen world, I need education, information, and sensitivity in light of God's descriptive and prescriptive Word.

But not every situation presents a moral dilemma. Some can be easily embraced now. And all of them will be brought under judgment. In that day there will be everlasting righteousness, even if the present moment stinks. The certainty of final truth being brought to every situation is a good reason to be thankful in every circumstance.

The fire of the Spirit should not be put out (v. 19), because I should count on real help, comfort, and correction. He will reveal the truth. He is the Advocate promised by Jesus. As he came to the disciples at Pentecost, so he will continue to work in his children. I am not a closed box or a finished person. There is still work being done on each of us. His help and direction are adding to what I am. We must be prepared to learn, to be jolted, and even to be made insecure for a moment. We must allow doubts and questions, for they lead us to better understandings.

For these reasons we must never assume that we know all there is to know (v. 20). As we go through life, new questions will arise. New problems will occur along the way. We will be faced with additional challenges. We will discover answers to questions we did not have before. These answers will be clear and often in places where we did not expect them. God's Word is not just written for a first reading. Any careful text, whether it is a contract, medical analysis, or love letter, deserves repeated and careful study.

A desire to know will often need to precede the discovery of knowledge. I must first recognize my need, even when I do not define it. Where death is seen as normal, the only comfort sought will be that of someone holding my hand. Where it is seen as a problem to be resolved, medicine will try to find ways to resist its harsh and cruel rule.

In the same way, oil under the ground was not discovered until there was a need for it. I also have frequently found that a new need brought to remembrance things I had read many times before and now understand in a new light. However, there is no magic in this. We are also prone to read into texts what we want to find in them. The greatest hindrance to knowledge is the belief that we already know. We do that with love letters when we want to be loved. We do that with contracts when we want to have things our way.

We do it with the Bible unless we hone our skill and approach it with the questions of real human existence to which we desire answers. Skillful readers will train themselves to see what the text says and what it does not say. They will understand that silence is as inspired as the text itself. For that reason, we are told to test everything (v. 21) and to hold on to the good. Spiritual hunger cannot replace the need for careful examination. The desire to know cannot be satisfied when we try to get knowledge by a shortcut. The confidence in the inspired Bible does not free us from careful word studies. Spirituality does not replace our minds and critically sharpened maturity.

When we proceed skillfully, we will be able to increasingly avoid every kind of evil (v. 22). We will still suffer pain, find life hard at times, annoy other people, and find them annoying us. We may wish for a different world or a different calling. We may have visions of greener grass on the other side of the fence. We may feel attracted to pack up everything and leave for more exotic regions.

God has tied himself down to a promise. We do have hope concerning what God will yet do in history, and therefore we do not grieve as those without hope. But we do grieve. George Frideric Handel composed an aria in which the main line is "Life is a pain." Right on! That is a central affirmation of the Christian worldview. But it does not end there.

Paul gave us a better ending in his letter to encourage the gutsy Christians he left in Thessalonica: "May God himself, the God of peace, sanctify you through and through. May your whole spirit, soul and body be kept blameless at the coming of our Lord Jesus Christ. The one who calls you is faithful and he will do it" (vv. 23–24).

8
The Samaritan Appeal

As soon as you get on the mailing list, you will receive appeals for help, pictures of needy people, and descriptions of projects you might or might not be interested in. There are so many children in need and abandoned people with their medical problems. There are drug therapy efforts and homes for people with disabilities, both here and abroad. There are natural disasters like floods, droughts, volcanic eruptions, and earthquakes. Large numbers of people are left homeless and without resources. There are refugees from political terror and civil war. And there are economic refugees hoping to find better conditions elsewhere.

Too many people around the world are in terrible straits and enormous pain through natural and human catastrophes. Tragedies result from the mismanagement of resources, widespread superstition, and occult religious practices—such as when the fields can only be planted after the stars line up in a certain way or only three days after the first full moon when the rains have finally stopped.

Physical factors play a role where there are few raw materials, irregular weather patterns, and a hostile climate. But, in addition, there is a whole range of often unimaginably inhuman beliefs about life and work, about social and political power instead of law, and about fate and spirits. There are also inhuman traditions and indoctrinations that adversely affect the way people live. These keep people from effectively managing to make a living.

Rarely are we exposed to the immediate situation of our fellow human beings in such conditions. Access to such information often needs to be thrown at us, since we have been able to insulate ourselves from the neighbor who has such problems and whose slice of life is filled with bitterness, pain, and isolation. In former times people were exposed to the full range of human suffering at home in their own contexts. Neighbors were born with disabilities or their disabilities resulted from an illness, from social upheaval, from war, or from natural catastrophe. Our modern securities, protective measures, and abilities shelter

The Samaritan Appeal

us from the harshest pain; but these factors have not long been in place.

Earlier generations had a short life expectancy because they were constantly exposed to illness and infections they did not understand. In addition, they knew little of the protection granted under law in a civil society. For the most part, they lived under the arbitrary rule of those in power. They were more victims of circumstances than masters of their situations. They had no one to appeal to other than God, or they just accepted whatever happened to them as part of their appointed destiny.

The rule of law—known to the Jews, imposed on England in the Magna Carta, and later exhibited in the Bill of Rights and similar documents—was only ever labored for in cultures influenced by Judaism and Christianity. The dominion over creation, a rational approach to the workings of nature, and a moral distinction between what is and what should be all came from the biblical worldview. It has been largely foreign to other cultures, except where they have come under the influence of European thought informed by Christianity, but not without conflict over traditional pagan patterns.

Most of us in Western societies are now quite sheltered from daily exposure to many of the horrible experiences and emergencies that are very common to the larger portion of the human race around the globe. On the good side of this, needy people actually can get care from the state and from private initiative and good works. The bad side is that it is easier to believe that all problems are solved and people in need either are at fault or are already being cared for. Often the largest budget items in Western governments are social projects, such as those for disability illness, special homes, rehabilitation, education, and unemployment insurance. These efforts seek to diminish suffering and to help people be integrated or at least be cared for. We provide for this through taxes, private initiatives, and benevolent donations.

But outside our narrow experience of the world, more needs to be done. Books, television reports, and eyewitness accounts tell us that more should be done to change the situation of the poor, needy, and hungry around the world or right next door. The problem is that so often it is an appeal to our wallet by way of our emotions at times of emergencies. A detailed study of the background of the emergency would be necessary to avoid recurrences, but there is no time for it then.

Most proposals for aid show a tragic ignorance of the basic economics of poverty and wealth as well as an unawareness of the influence of antihuman cultural and religious practices. In fact, the latter factors are often deliberately ignored. They would require cultural change after a critical study of inhuman pagan religions and their views of society. Instead, you view pictures of women with children on their backs laboring to get firewood, men herding their emaciated animals, and children with extended bellies—all without an explanation of why such conditions persist after decades of aid, scientific knowledge, grants, and government or private investments.

An appeal to your pocket by way of your emotions is also found among Christians with an emphasis on sharing things, food, and clothing, mostly without the concomitant emphasis on sharing ideas and worldviews as well. Such appeals rarely reflect the fact that there is no miracle of Christ in the Bible without an accompanying sermon explaining the why and what of God's miraculous action. Folders and pamphlets in the mail encourage Christians to work "miracles" of unselfishness in their own lives through giving more. But most relief efforts then fail to deliver the necessary sermon along with the goods to those in need. They also should review the cultural and social practices to avoid repeated suffering. One large international relief agency even says that the sharing of funds and food are the "signs and wonders" of God in our time, that they parallel the work of God in the book of Acts.

The story of the Good Samaritan (Luke 10:25–37) is often told as a reminder of the selfish acts of the priest and the Levite who, seeing the man by the roadside between Jerusalem and Jericho, walked past him. Both saw his wounds, must have heard his groaning, and saw him beaten and robbed of his clothes. Yet they felt no stirring of national, religious, or human commonality and walked past him without lending a hand. Perhaps they were scared that they might also be robbed if they stopped to help. More likely they had their religious and national filters through which they justified their noninvolvement. Here was a man in need, but then, he was not one of theirs.

At last a Samaritan came by. He was moved with compassion and stopped to wash the wounds with alcohol (wine) to disinfect them and to sooth them with oil. Then he placed the suffering man on his own animal, walked him to the nearest inn, and there gave orders that the innkeeper should take care of the victim at the Samaritan's expense. He promised to return and pay whatever extra was required in the days to come.

This man, according to both the questioning Jew and Jesus, was the true neighbor to the fallen man. Beyond all distinctions, common humanity calls for intervention of the able on behalf of the weak.

It is a good story to make us all feel guilty, challenged, and shocked; for we recognize that we are all neighbors in the one human race. It is a good story then to move us to action, to urge us to get involved to help those in need by the side of the roads we walk on throughout our lives. There are those beaten by circumstances of geography, politics, poor health, ignorance, and false religions.

I do not live in a world in which the neighbors are all my friends. Nor do I live in a world in which I can rest in affirming my goodness, since all social needs are met by the

The Samaritan Appeal

taxes I pay to the state, which then makes the right, wise, and efficient choices about how to help the people in need in my community. The more funds raised through taxation, the less I feel burdened by the remaining needs. My share is already so great.

Yet there continue to be situations in which I am personally required to assist, on the spur of the moment, in the immediate needs of others, when I can diminish the suffering of the neighbor.

It is interesting that Luke places this debate with the vivid illustration or teaching tool of the Good Samaritan story right before the description of the gathering of Jesus in the home of Martha and Mary. They were friends of the Lord and had him in their home a number of times. They called him when their brother Lazarus died (John 11) and celebrated together when he had been raised again. At that time (John 12), Mary even broke the perfume jar over Jesus' feet and anointed him with the nard in full wonder and appreciation for the Lord's power and kindness to them.

But here in Luke 10:38–42 both sisters were being hostesses in Martha's house when Mary sat down at Jesus' feet to listen to his words. We are not told what they talked about, but it must have been centrally important because Mary did not want to miss a word of it. Martha, as the older sister and owner of the house, was so busy preparing all kinds of things that she was not able to get it all done. She was distracted with much serving. And then the Lord told her that what Mary was doing was the more necessary thing to do—she was listening to the Lord.

I don't think that we can see this as the Lord's distinction of importance between material and spiritual food, or between temporal and eternal interests, or between body and soul. Many Christians do read it that way. But this kind of distinction is introduced from a Hellenistic and Platonic view of Christianity and dismisses the rightful pleasure of God in his material world, in his lunch with Abraham, and in Jesus' eating with sinners. This distinction also overlooks the divine command to practice hospitality as a Christian concern.

Instead, I find it most interesting that Luke puts the priority of listening to the Lord immediately after the account of the Good Samaritan. The cry for help, the need to love neighbors as ourselves, and the reminder that we are all part of one human race that lives in a world of robbers all need to be brought into connection with a dependence on God's Word to tell us how we should love neighbors and be of help to people in need.

Circumstances themselves do not give us wisdom on what is the right solution. Higher taxes do not, by themselves, mean better social services. An alcoholic does not need another bottle. Individuals caught in the results of African tribal religions need more than just a helping hand. They also need to have their worldview changed—their thinking about

The Samaritan Appeal

God and human beings, about nature and life, and about work and death. The spontaneity of the Samaritan is right toward a person who is faced so closely with real danger or even death. But to get the needy out of similar situations in the future may well require moral and intellectual help and a new spiritual orientation to prevent entrapment in the same situation again.

Physical need requires physical assistance. But where physical need is the result of inhuman values and practices, there is also a need for a powerful change in ideas and choices. This is a repeated biblical emphasis. Ideas make an obvious contribution for better or worse in the lives and histories of all people around the world. Many want to overlook the relation between ideas and practice, but when the heart and mind are not changed, the old problems and inabilities will persist.

So Luke placed into the immediate context the priority of listening to the Lord. Mary needed to learn from him who is the eternal Creator what life is all about and how and why it was created. Mary needed to know why things don't work out, why the Samaritans despised Jesus (Luke 9:51–56), and what place life, love, and leisure have in a broken world. Only the Creator could sufficiently explain the whence, what, and whither of human existence.

Operating without a biblical perspective leads to so much waste. The appeal from Christians to be humble, to share, to consume less, and to just believe and trust is met with a warm response, whether driven by guilt or generosity. Especially in the North American experience, people tend to be more openly generous, partially out of their Christian background and partially out of their own historical experience.

I recently met a Greek man who owns a diner. He was being very gentle with a Russian student waiter, explaining things over and over to her in his immigrant accent. Her language skills were very poor, but she was trying. Turning to us, he commented that he had also started out that way when he first came over from the old country. He commented on the generous help he had then received.

What people actually do out of generosity is often immense and surprising. There is an amazing amount of goodwill, of compassion, and of wishing to help others overcome their miserable situations. When pictures arrive of starving people, of houses crushed by earthquakes or floods, of lives destroyed by war or fire, the amount of donated funds, of time given, and of materials shipped is amazing. Donating blood, medicine, clothes, vacation time, and professional skills is not left to a few or always to the same people. Many from all walks of life step in to help others who may be total strangers, yet who benefit rapidly from the voluntary contributions.

Yet a great deal of such donations affects little beyond the immediate need. It does not change much beyond the immediate catastrophe. Often it has little lasting effect on the lives, thoughts, and practices of the people helped. One reason is

The Samaritan Appeal

that the recipients do not understand it. They welcome the material help to change their material situation but do not grasp that it is also an investment intended to change habits, values, and priorities. Their minds have not comprehended from what specific outlook such surplus of things comes. They easily accept the ideas familiar to us from both Marxism and materialism (and often propagated by Christians) that surplus only comes from prior theft. The goods then come as an act of redistribution or repentance for past evil. They assume that we have more only because we have stolen it in the first place and have come to repay a debt.

Left out of this equation is the intellectual, spiritual, and cultural contribution to wealth that Christianity has made based on the teachings of God's Word. Mary did well to sit at the feet of the Lord in order to listen to his word. The man found by the side of the road, beaten and robbed, does well to understand from God that we do not live in a safe world, but in one of robbers, thieves, and death. We do not live in a world in which we can assume that all people are kind, lawful, and honest. Reality after the fall is a dangerous place. Cain killed Abel from jealousy. Authoritarian governments everywhere resent the freedoms Christianity brought to the Western world.

They even resent the message of such freedoms carried into their realms through products and people. Around the globe, envy of the wealth of the Western world—wherever its people settled—prevents the desire to learn how and why they have largely managed to perform better, use resources more wisely, and solve problems more effectively through science, education, and personal efforts. Behind much of the tragedy of the world lies the hideous manipulation of lives away from the knowledge of the God of the Bible and everything that relates to his really being there. The obsession and envy against the best elements of Jewish and Christian culture are a resentment against people being free to work, think, debate, and create—all of which are mandated in Genesis, at the very beginning of the Bible.

All religions—whether secular, as in dialectical materialism, or religious, as in Islam, Buddhism, African tribal religions, and animism—urge the person to fit in, to submit, and to go with the flow. The collective in one cultural and philosophical context is paralleled in another by the call to communal obedience and in a third by detachment from anything that hints of humans having individual personhood. Nirvana is a rather selfish goal of becoming indifferent to the tragic and unconcerned about a neighbor or an individual's own obligation to be a person.

Only the Bible calls each of us by a name, urges us to stand and to work with our hands and minds to have dominion over the earth, and tells us to resist evil after the fall of Adam and Eve. This is not due to our being a better race; there is only one race—the human race. But it is due largely

The Samaritan Appeal

to the fact that through the centuries the Word of God gave shape to a different mindset, different priorities, and different habits. It is a matter of an effort for humane culture, chosen over the experience of mere human nature.

Interestingly, the next passage in Luke's Gospel talks about how this knowledge from the Creator is accessible. The passage gives us what is known as the Lord's Prayer (Luke 11:1–4). Although we cannot sit at the feet of Jesus as Mary did in her lifetime, we still have access to the source of all life and wisdom. As the Lord's Prayer tells us, we have a Father in heaven, whom we may and should address in all confidence and trust. His Word tells us that we are his children, for he intentionally made us. We are not the result of chance in whatever amount of time. We are persons in his image. And because God is a person who thinks, feels, and acts, we do those things as well since he made us in his image.

To him we may come because his name is hallowed. Our focus initially is on God, who is holy. That means that he is specific, trustworthy, consistent, and distinct in his characteristics. The God of the Bible is not an arbitrary God. He is not the unknown God of the Athenians, of Emmanuel Kant, or of much modern theology that denies the Bible is the Word of God. So we set his name apart, for we know he is our Maker, and we know his favor toward us.

Imagine for a moment that it were not so. You would not know what is on God's mind. He might be powerful but not faithful, good, and gracious in his character. Or he might be weak, perhaps one among a myriad of gods and spirits found in pagan contexts in India, Africa, and parts of South America. Or perhaps he might be one of the spirits that are honored by prayer cloths that flutter in the wind from bushes and trees along the roads and lakeshores of Asia. There would never be a reason to hallow any one of these deities.

But our God has a kingdom on the way. It will come because he is King and at work. We long for that kingdom, and we already work in our choices and creativity to advance it forcefully through being human, creative, kind, just, and willing to serve what is right and good.

The hope for the kingdom of God is not a futuristic dream or a kind of make-believe in order to be able to justify a general optimism. Rather, it is tied to our recognition that we live in a created, not random, universe. We know that we live after the fall of Adam. We also know that God is at work to restore all things, which he has shown through the express clarifications about all of life in the Bible and through the raising of Christ with a real body in real history.

In the first three lines of the Lord's Prayer, we acknowledge God. Our focus is on him. We remember who made us and who our gracious Redeemer is. We ground ourselves again in this confidence. We know we are not just talking to the ceiling or the thin air beyond, nor are we guessing things about God. We are not addressing something in the hope that some spirit might just be passing by then. No, we address our Father in heaven, whose name is hallowed and whose kingdom will come.

Then we focus on ourselves. We are needy people in body and in mind. We are not self-made, self-contained, or self-defined. So we talk to our heavenly Father about our basic needs. We need bread (food and drink) because our minds and souls need healthy bodies to express and do what is good and right.

We are also messed up and confused. We are not perfect in any area. We have sinned and live in a world in which other people add to our problems. So we ask God to help us, to forgive us our sin and give us courage to forgive others who have sinned against us and recognized it. As in all forgiveness, this is not a matter of wiping out the guilt, but of choosing to respond with gracious "forth-giving" whenever we are asked to pardon, rather than harboring a desire for vengeance.

We also ask God that, in the times ahead, we would not be in the specific kind of tough situations in which we would easily yield to temptations. Temptations, however, surround as at all times. As soon as we have a choice, in fact or in our imaginations, we are tempted. All creativity results from choices, and only when there is a choice can we love, obey, and create or neglect, disobey, and destroy. Yielding to the latter options when they are wrong, irrational, or idealistic and playing with them in our minds or through our actions brings about sin—that is the problem. Christ was tempted in all things as we are, yet he did not sin in any one of them.

We pray then that in life's many opportunities we would choose what is good and right. For that, we ask for wisdom, the kind of discernment that enables us to anticipate the results of whatever choice we make. Often, right and wrong, wise and foolish become clear when we consider what the result will be. We ask God to keep us from situations in which such insight is not yet available and from situations in which we are too tired to remember, too pressed to be wise, too naive to know enough, or too much in love to remember that a lifetime is a very long time for any commitment.

The sequence of these three passages in Luke gives us the help we need to deal with the kind of situations we have been discussing in this book. We face a world of problems. There is what someone called a free-floating guilt attributed to many of us, because problems still exist in the world while we are reasonably healthy, wealthy, perhaps even wise, and at least educated.

The model most often presented of what a just and caring society would look like is one in which everyone would have the same amount of everything: food, health, money, income, vacations, and transportation.

Yet we should recognize that this is only a mathematical egalitarianism. There are people who think and work, and there are those who don't. This fact must not be disregarded.

Socialism tried the enforced collective in which people were regarded only as numbers. But, of course, numbers don't work or weep or take or reject responsibility. The difference between people is, to a large extent, the result of the different ideas they have about the basic building blocks of life itself. These ideas are rooted in their ways of looking at the world around them. Their worldviews influence their choices, deeds, priorities, health, relationships, and governments.

Therefore, the mere pursuit of a mathematical equality is unjust because of the different things people believe and do. It assumes that the outcome should always be the same whatever you do. Yet this will never happen, as Marxist socialism has demonstrated again and again. Remember the Russian proverb I referred to above: "We pretend to work and they pretend to pay us." Where there is no reward—because the state or the boss steals it or because initiative is not encouraged by fatalistic religions—people will see no value in working hard.

We live in a wounded world. People are robbed like the poor man by the road between Jerusalem and Jericho. What are we to do? We need to be a neighbor to him and give what we have of attention, care, and funds in the immediate emergency situation. But then we also need to remember Christ's words about life in the real world. What did God have in mind when he made us? Why is it such a mess now? How are we going to resist evil, false laws, false religions and their worldviews, bacteria in the sick, and weather patterns that bring rain only twice a year in one part of the world and too much at once in another?

God's words in the Bible give wisdom, practical examples, and intelligent advice for being creative in defying adverse natural circumstances. Nature, including human nature, needs to be transformed into culture.

On the basis of this prayer taught by Jesus and the whole Bible, we can confidently pray to the Father, expressing our understanding of how worthy he is to be trusted. We admire, hallow, and single out his being, character, and name. We long for his kingdom to come here on earth among people so they all would see the one and true God of reality and understand the purpose of our being human.

Postscript

At the close of this book we are profoundly aware of both the greatness of human beings and their often tragically limited means of coping with adverse conditions. Human beings are amazing. That statement is easily a common observation about the human family. Whatever our circumstances, we seek and often find ways to make life a bit more tolerable, colorful, imaginative. At the same time, there are very difficult situations. Many of these are the result of geography or natural conditions and have been addressed by other writers. My interest lies more in the area of ideas, what people think and believe about the world they live and work in. For I believe that what a person thinks about the building blocks of his situation will stimulate or restrain action and intervention to change the prevalent conditions.

The building blocks I have in mind are the philosophical/religious beliefs and the moral/cultural practices in relation to the real world we inhabit. Our social customs, our chains of authority, our attitudes toward the human mind and knowledge are such blocks. Also central is the question of how I approach that real world and the people in it. Do I have an attitude of doubt or acceptance? Do I see the world that is there or an imagined one? Do I regard it from the perspective of its rightfulness, normality, and inevitability, or do I look at it, because of experienced pain and conflict, from the perspective of its possible imperfection and the subsequent need to fix it?

In the preceding chapters I wanted in no way to raise one person above another or diminish the dignity of anyone as a human being. There is a wonderful amount of variation, of creative ways to liven up things, to dance at a wedding, to eat, and to play. There are various ways to harness water, to till the land, to make use of other forms of power than merely the human hand.

But there is also a common form to our lives. We are all born into a world without having been asked. That world already had a shape, which we inherited. In addition, we were born into a cultural, social, legal, and religious context we also had no choice over. There is no merit in being from here rather than there, in living now or in the past, in being male or female and in having our specific parents as mother and father.

Such factors precede and shape us. They are the givens of our world. We begin life within the framework set by the conditions and choices of earlier generations. But we are people, not sticks or stones, not just genetic information chains or lumps of matter. We all have our own set of choices to weigh and to make. It helps that from an early stage of child development we discover our own abilities to question and to argue, to play along or to resist. We learn language as a tool to communicate and then use it also to deceive. We discover the distinction between a fact and a fable, between truth and deception, and we learn to laugh at, mock, and butter up people. At an early age we discover the need to figure things out, since the world of things is full of unknown wonders and dangers and the world of people is full of helpful and harmful folk.

But soon the drive to pull away, to question, to discover, and to be ourselves gets absorbed into the easier path to go along, to conform, and to be liked and admitted. This hampers the earlier age of discovery. What could have been a way toward responsible intellectual freedom becomes a path to resignation, wishing not to rock the boat. When Jesus speaks of becoming like little children he does not admonish us to be silent, compliant, and group-oriented. Instead he blames adults for no longer having the unabashed courage to question, to demand answers, to doubt, and to discover what is true about God and human life. Adults are ashamed to stick out; for the child, it is a part of normal curiosity. And only the curious, who seek with all their heart and mind, will find and recognize the value of what they found.

It is remarkable, however, that many are not always satisfied with conformity. It is wonderful that people are not consistent with their fatalism, their decision to give up. The Soviet State, though based on dialectic materialism, recognized the latent danger in human minds and tried to punish them. People were not satisfied with history or nature or science being the final mover. They wanted to think for themselves. They knew that without open discussions Marxism was neither a dialectic system or materialistic, since the whole thing was an idea in the minds of the Soviet 'Trinity' of Hegel, Marx, and Lenin.

There are other inconsistencies in what people suggest as ways to understand the world around us. Any relativist has to be absolutist about his relativism to even get a hearing. The Zen master has to have a disciple to explain in words the meaning of his silence. The proposition of modern theology that God is the *totaliter aliter* or 'wholly other,' about whom nothing definitive can be said, attempts to be a definitive statement about the being and nature of God. Then again, any view that the present is the best of all possible worlds, whether coming from Marxists, Christians, or traditionalists, has no way to explain the tears from grief and sorrow over obvious imperfections.

Such inconsistencies enable some to raise questions. They stand out and make trouble. The Marxist State used police to check the thinking of people. Islam threatens death to the unbeliever. The violator of African tribal traditions will be chased out of the village or poisoned because he is unlike the believing group. The system works only in the abstract. In the real world people and their lives are untidy, exactly what the Bible describes: people think, evaluate, are full of good and bad ideas, reflect, and doubt; and life is always unfinished.

We are thankful for the troublemaker who dares to tell the emperor that he has no clothes, that a tradition is inhuman, that a religion does not encourage human existence. The prophets accused the normality of immoral behavior. Jesus argued with religious leaders. The challenges from an opposition party may lead to better governance.

Wherever in the world I traveled for my work, I met people addressing their issues, conflicts, and challenges with much ingenuity. Human beings do not only exist or pass through biological phases. We also worry and complain; we work and accomplish much. Most of the time mothers and fathers care for their children. Parents worry about health and education, about safety and survival. We single out our bed or cot; we turn a coke can into a toy; and we plant a vine next to our door to mark our uniqueness and to complain against the merely common. We choose recipes, wear clothes, listen and laugh; we keep some thoughts to ourselves; we are better off and safer when we initially doubt—all these practices express our distinct humanity. Men and women chat, discuss, argue; they whisper or they shout; they like to please and often judge too easily. The many ways in which a human being is unlike natural phenomena and unpredictable in his or her next choice expresses that wonder I have experienced often in strange places: These people are of my kind.

I have also experienced much sadness, horror, and shock over people's cruelty to each other, rough treatment, neglect, quick judgment without remorse or grace, and despondency when normality in a person's life is seen as binding him or her to an inevitable condition. For when everything in life is seen as already decided by God or materially caused or subject to the will and power of some higher being or older tradition, change, review, and alternatives are almost unthinkable. Ideas shape our intellectual and moral landscape. They may grow in the fertile soil of Christianity or emanate from the rocky sterility of a moonscape. The Jew and the Christian has a word from the infinite-personal God of the Bible that tells him to stand up, think and critique, and then do. Outside of this view people hear the cry for collective submission to gods, fate, nature, or custom: In every case, lie low and make do until death.

Postscript

Human beings really have only a few options to understand their place in reality, in the time and space of history. One either begins with the impersonal thing and ends as a victim of circumstances, without anyone's will, purpose, or moral mandate; or one begins with a personal being who is mindful of the way things should work and invites us to choose between options, alternatives, and even life or death. All religions contain the first option, whether they are materialistic or spiritual. The individual must join the collective, the doubter must become a believer, the present bears the face of the old. What is has always been, and what is normal is, well, just normal.

Religions offer a way of seeing our life as part of a flow. We are particles of the way things are anyway. They help us take root and fit in. They describe pretty much what is normal and urge us to join, to follow, to obey, to repeat, . . . and to shut up. When all people shout in a chorus, there is none outside to answer. Everything follows a necessity, whether from the weight of celestial bodies on our psyche, or our genetic make-up, or the flow of an inevitable history. It is philosophically not important whether the control is material or divine, whether Marx or Mohammed teach it, whether the flow comes from traditions or from the hope of future bliss here on earth or in heaven beyond.

The Bible gives a philosophical framework for the existence of people with a choice and with such a damaged reality.

Its initial proposition about a personal God is about someone who is eternal and thinks, who is powerful to create and full of emotions, and who delights in both order and variety, rule and imagination. According to that viewpoint people are there because they are made in the image of that God with a mandate to create, to invent, to explore, to talk and discuss. Things have gone wrong sinc then, but initially our home is not a cold, impersonal everything, but a personal being: Father, Son, and Holy Spirit.

That proposition about God and the creature made in the image of God gives rise to everything that we value in human beings. While religions demean people by binding them to conformity, Judaism and Christianity give responsibility to freely love, create, enjoy, and improve real life. Even sinful human beings have the mandate to work against what they have done, provoked, and all now painfully experience.

Things can and did go terribly wrong when that freedom was misused to believe a lie. How can anyone believe they could be like God, or that people are now perfect, or that death is just another experience the living will go through, or that human beings are not really different but are conditioned by gender, genetics, or geography to behave the way they do?

The Bible, or rather the God of the Bible, the human being of the Bible, and the history described in the Bible give us the only coherent insight into significant, purposeful existence.

Postscript

Because of the repeated proposition, many generations of Jews and Christians understood something of the uniqueness of Biblical viewpoints. We have inherited a worldview that is not fatalistic, unquestionable, inevitable, or finally inhuman. That teaching produced cultural changes. People began to see themselves in a different light, with real responsibilities to work, live, and seek justice. Under the effect of that teaching we no longer have genuine Vandals of the original kind. You would be hard pressed to find a Goth, a Lombard, a Viking, or an Allemande. They were there, roaming across Europe and raping, pillaging, and generally making mischief, until the teaching from the heart of the monasteries conquered their minds, created sensible laws, and changed their lives.

The developing rule of law, the spread of education, the conquest of disease through medicines, a fair justice system, trade and skills, the voyages of discovery, scientific research and manufacturing, the bill of rights, and the equality of men and women all have their intellectual and cultural foundation in the teaching of Christianity. Because Christians admittedly are not by definition only nice people, much mischief was also done. Increasing knowledge also gives power, and we all recognize that absolute power corrupts absolutely. Visions of grandeur perverted the call to servanthood. Socialism (both the national socialism of Hitler and the international socialist program of Stalin and his friends) destroyed civil societies. For many years Christians were not immune against the temptation of copying slave traders in Africa and Arabia, until more sensitive Christians labored to abolish it and to talk about universal human rights.

Out of our Christian and Jewish insights we acknowledge that great problems persist around the world. Particular to that insight is the perspective of the possible abnormality of things, which then opens eyes to recognize problems for what they are. If this world is normal, nothing should be or needs to be done about it. Only where problems are singled out are solutions explored and applied. That mindset was brought to us from Jerusalem and confirmed what Athens was thinking about but could not resolve. It spread from the church to the city, from monasteries to the surrounding land, from universities to rulers and people. In the modern world minds and hearts need to once again be changed by the clearer insight gained from Biblical realism. Cultures must be celebrated in the non-essential patterns of local tastes. But they must be invited to consider change in matters relating to life in the real world, where social habits, forms of government, the rule of law, people's work, property rights, and genuine individuality of persons need to be brought in line with that reality. That change may require the review and possibly the breaking of religious bonds and tribal customs.

The greatest form of poverty is the poverty of mind, of ideas, of understanding the real world. Resources are not only found in lucky places, they can also be created and multiplied when needs are recognized and means are established to alleviate them. And the greatest resource is the human mind. Here solutions are invented and alternatives thought through; here the will is strengthened to not be a victim of circumstances but a fellow-creator with God to repair in stages the brokenness of his world.